'Excellent. Thoroughly contemporary. Thoroughly biblical.
And the intersection of the two is mind-blowing. In a day
when Christians so often simply baptize the latest trends
in secular psychology, this book is refreshingly biblical,
genuinely life-changing, a great model of Christian
thinking. Here is the word of God reviving the soul.
Here is good news. Here is freedom.'
Tim Chester, church leader and author

'This is a fantastic little gem! And important not only for
young adults openly struggling with issues of identity and
image, but also for all of us bombarded with worldly
measures of success and failure. And especially church
leaders. Graham urges us to "look into the mirror" of
Scripture to understand ourselves. What emerges is the
simple, healthy principle of "humble dignity". Having
skilfully analysed the worldly components of our distorted
self-image in appearance, success and status, he traces with
crystal clarity the Bible's teaching about our humanity, from
our creation in the image of God through the gospel of
grace and acceptance in Christ to our hope of the new
creation. The last chapters are stunning: liberating
applications of the gospel to issues of self-worth, praise and
criticism, success and failure, relationships and appearance. I
came to the book assuming that it was for a few anxious
youngsters. I discovered that I needed it. I finished it

wanting all our staff, home-groups and teenagers to study it. This is biblical medicine for healing our souls so sick with self-obsession – deeply perceptive, easy to read, hugely practical and wonderfully reassuring of our humble dignity in Christ.'
Richard Coekin, Senior Pastor of the Co-Mission Initiative, SW London

'Challenging and encouraging! Perfect for people wanting to explore their identity in Christ, and what that means to their life.'
Lizzie Glover, nineteen-year-old student

ivp

Graham Beynon

mirror

Discover your true identity in Christ

INTER-VARSITY PRESS
Norton Street, Nottingham NG7 3HR, England
Email: ivp@ivpbooks.com
Website: www.ivpbooks.com

First published 2008

British Library Cataloguing in Publication Data
A catalogue record for this book is available from the British Library.

ISBN: 978-1-84474-325-4

Set in Monotype Dante 12/15pt
Typeset in Great Britain by Servis Filmsetting Ltd, Stockport, Cheshire
Printed and bound in Great Britain by Ashford Colour Press Ltd, Gosport,
Hampshire

Inter-Varsity Press publishes Christian books that are true to the Bible
and that communicate the gospel, develop discipleship and strengthen the
church for its mission in the world.

Inter-Varsity Press is closely linked with the Universities and Colleges
Christian Fellowship, a student movement connecting Christian Unions
in universities and colleges throughout Great Britain, and a member
movement of the International Fellowship of Evangelical Students.
Website: www.uccf.org.uk

contents

foreword

Facebook and MySpace are fascinating. I love clicking through people's profile pictures. You can get a real sense of what someone's like as you look through their biog or photos. You may even be surprised that the Trekkie in your home-group was actually the European off-road quad biking champion!

But have you ever wondered about what your profile page says about you? Why you chose one photo as your profile picture over another? Why you omitted to share with the world that your favourite films are all chick flicks . . . even though you're a very manly five-a-side player?

When I chat to the students I work with about this, what we come back to is that we want to portray an image of ourselves to the world. We want to be seen in a certain way. Or we want to see ourselves in a certain way. And sometimes, when someone holds a mirror up to us, we don't like what we see.

Mirror, Mirror deals with one of the most-asked questions and least-understood areas in Christian living. Image. Identity. Self-esteem. How does being a Christian impact what I see when I stand in front of the mirror? Whether this is an area you are struggling with yourself or you are seeking to help others, you'll find Graham's wisdom invaluable.

There's a bit of desert out there in Christian thinking on the area of self-image. Often the advice falls into one of two camps. Either the L'Oréal camp, 'you're worth it' (because Jesus thinks you're special), or the Pond Scum camp, 'you're a nasty, unworthy sinner' – neither of which really shows the balance of Scripture, and neither of which really helps us to have a healthy view of ourselves.

I hope you'll find *Mirror, Mirror* an oasis, as I did. Graham has a pastor's heart. He loves the people he cares for in his church (you'll see that in each and every chapter) and he loves God's life-giving word. He'll help you discover a refreshing and biblical framework about what it means to be truly human.

You'll find his concept of 'humble dignity' can be applied to all sorts of situations – whether you are having a 'fat day' as you go through the wardrobe like a woman possessed, or you're avoiding talking to a friend about a difficult issue. It's a concept that helps us live and breathe 24/7 what it means to be 'in Christ', and not just on a Sunday.

So, whether you are looking to help others in their discipleship, wanting to start thinking more deeply about this area, or you want to find some personal applications for yourself, get reading.

You might even change your profile picture . . .

Linda Marshall
UCCF Midlands Team Leader

preface

It all started with a phone call from Mike who worked in student ministry. He wanted me to do a training day for some of his staff and the topic he had chosen was self-image. 'But I don't know anything about self-image,' I protested. 'But it's really important,' he argued.

He went on to explain that he'd asked his staff for the most common topics they ended up talking to students about, or areas where they thought students struggled. The top two were relationships and self-image. 'And we've got some good books and material on relationships, but nothing on self-image,' he went on.

And so I ended up studying the Bible on self-image, and reading as widely as I could on the topic. I found it fascinating. I quickly realized it wasn't simply about helping people who might have a low self-image; that was only scratching the surface. It was much more about our identity, who we think we are, and who we really are in Christ. And I started to see loads of implications for how we should live and think of ourselves as a result.

I finally presented a day's seminar on the topic. My thinking had changed even by the end of that day. And my thinking continued to develop as I read more, thought more, discussed more, and did some more seminars. The end result (so far) is contained in these pages.

There are a variety of people to thank.

Eleanor Trotter, my editor at IVP, has been consistently encouraging and helpful in the whole process, from idea to finished manuscript.

There are the many people I have listened to or whose material I have read on this topic. Any helpful ideas, insights or illustrations I ever came across were gratefully stolen. Many of the sources of these are acknowledged in the pages that follow. Some aren't, but that is only because I no longer even know where they originally came from.

I must thank my church – Avenue Community Church in Leicester. The congregation and my fellow leaders have been encouraging and supportive of my writing. In addition I led a series of seminars on this topic and those who came willingly filled in feedback sheets each time. They openly and honestly shared some of their struggles, questions and reflections. Some of those thoughts appear in this book as quotes from individuals. I have taken the liberty of changing people's names and, on occasion, merging people's words. This is only for the sake of clarity and illustration, and I trust it remains true to the real lives represented. I am very grateful for the willingness of this group to share in this way and hope that these reflections are a help to those who read this book.

I must also thank those who read a draft version of the manuscript for this book and fed back invaluable comments. My thinking and writing is richer and more balanced as a result of their input. They were Paula Love, Julian Hardyman, Julie Kite, Gordon Dalzell, Dan Hames, Linda Marshall and my wife Charis.

This book is dedicated to Charis. I've written a few books and we've occasionally joked about when I would dedicate one to her. Well, here it is – and it's only appropriate that it is a book on our identity because she more than anyone else has helped me know who I am in Christ. Later pages will speak about how God has loved and accepted us despite ourselves. It is that love and acceptance from God that Charis has mirrored to me.

Graham Beynon
March 2008

1. looking in the mirror

On Saturday evenings at our house you will often find me watching a film with our three children. Fortunately we've moved beyond the *Thomas the Tank Engine Chugs Again*-type stuff on to higher-quality animation films. The more sophisticated ones usually operate on two levels. That's the case with the film *Antz*, about a colony of, you guessed it, ants.

The opening scene has the lead character 'Z', voiced by Woody Allen, lying on a psychiatrist's couch talking to his counsellor. While the children watching the film might not pick it up, the adults soon realize this scene is hitting all the classic buttons about self-image. The conversation goes like this:

> Z: I think everything must go back to the fact that I had a very anxious childhood. My mother never had time for me. You know when you're the middle child in a family of five million, you don't get any attention. I mean how's it possible?

And I've always had these abandonment issues which plague me. My Father was basically a drone like I've said, you know the guy flew away when I was just a larva.

And my job, don't get me started on it because it really annoys me. I was not cut out to be a 'worker', I tell you right now. I feel physically inadequate; my whole life I've never been able to lift more than ten times my own body weight. And when you get down to it, handling dirt is not my idea of a rewarding career.

It's this whole gung-ho super-organism thing that I can't get, you know I try but I don't get it. I'm supposed to do everything for the colony, but what about my needs, what about me? . . . The whole system makes me feel insignificant.

Counsellor: Excellent! You've made a real breakthrough.

Z: I have?

Counsellor: Yes Z, you are insignificant!

Z: I am?

It's a great scene. And it could have been taken from a case study of someone who has low self-image. There's the negative influence of our childhood and how our parents treated us; there's our body-image and how it matches up to what is considered 'normal'; there's our work experience and how dignified we think it is; there's the tension between my responsibilities to others and my needs being met. But ultimately there's the issue of *significance*.

This takes us straight to the topic of this book: Who do we think we are? How should we view ourselves? What significance do we have?

I should say straight away that this is not simply a book about self-image. I'm going to use that term a lot over the next few chapters and I'm going to do so because I think it's a useful way in to thinking about this topic. But the actual topic is much broader and deeper. It's about our identity. It's about how we define ourselves – how we know who we are.

The issue of our day

This is an issue that all people have been plagued by, and wrestled with, down the centuries. We have constantly asked, 'Who am I?' But it has become a modern obsession. Our culture is so preoccupied with feeling good about ourselves. We read about it in lifestyle magazines, ask questions about it in agony aunt columns, hear it in the lyrics of songs, and see it portrayed on TV.

It is almost everywhere in advertising. I saw an advert for face cream just this week, proudly announcing, 'It's All About Looking Good and Feeling Great.' It went on to assure us, 'Of course: the better we look, the better we feel.' Or what about the car advert that said, 'When you buy a new car, you buy a new part of yourself'? The implication is clearly that you are defined by your car, at least in part. So you can always improve your life by buying a better model (and preferably the one they are selling).

Elsewhere we're told that having bought this product, you'll feel better about yourself, or that you'll magically adopt the image conveyed in the advert: we are sold an image along with our shampoo. Or adverts simply appeal directly to our sense of worth – buy this product, we're told, 'Because you're worth it'.

In fact it's often assumed that having a low self-image is the great evil of our day. It has been blamed for everything from poor achievement at school to anti-social behaviour. Talk to anyone involved in education or community development and it usually isn't long before they mention the need to develop people's self-image.

One writer puts it like this:

> . . . incantations for self-worth, self-love and self-acceptance ooze
> out of the TV tube, drift across the radio waves, and entice
> through advertising. From the cradle to the grave, self-promoters
> promise to cure all of society's ills through doses of self-esteem,
> self-worth, self-acceptance and self-love. And everyone or nearly
> everyone echoes the refrain: 'You just need to love and accept
> yourself the way you are.'

And it isn't simply in the secular world that a high self-image is
seen as the solution to all our problems. In the Christian world
it's often touted in the same way. One leading Christian psych-
ologist, for example, wrote the following words:

> If I could write a prescription for the women of the world, I would
> provide each one of them with a healthy dose of self-esteem and
> personal worth (taken three times a day until symptoms
> disappear). I have no doubt that this is their greatest need.

He is writing specifically of women, but according to many
within the church, exactly the same could be said of Christian
men.

A painful issue

Of course we are not just talking about a current issue within
our culture and within the church. This is a very real and
painful issue for individuals. Just hear the anguish in the
following words:

> There it was again: an all too familiar voice . . . that so
> convincingly portrays me as small, inadequate, undesirable,
> insignificant. Why do I hate myself so much sometimes?

Some of the statistics are frightening, especially for teen-agers. It's reported that 75% of twelve- to seventeen-year-old girls would like cosmetic surgery because they would then feel happier about their appearance. Similarly 84% of teenage boys thought that having a better body would improve their lives.

As we grow older some of the angst we often feel about stuff like appearance may ease off (although not always!). But most of us are still concerned about some aspect of our image. It might be body image, career, sporting ability, status or hobbies. We define ourselves by how we look, what we wear, what we do, how successful we are, who we are with and so on. Those who are older can even go on to define themselves by the relative successes of their children.

An issue for everyone

For some people this issue of self-image is clearly much more of a 'problem'. They are down on themselves, they feel inad-equate and insignificant, and they assume that everyone else sees them as such. Their feelings of self-worth, or the lack of it, are a constant source of angst.

But what about the person who is confident and happy with who they are, even proud of themselves and their achievements? Christian counsellor and writer Ed Welch warns that the person who doesn't feel they have a problem with self-image may have the most dangerous version of it. He says: 'Such people feel they have made it. They have more than other people. They feel good about themselves. But their lives are still defined by other people [rather] than by God.'

These people are operating the same way as everyone else – thinking about where they are on the various ladders of success, beauty, popularity and status. It just so happens they think they are far enough up the ladder to feel OK about themselves, whereas people who have a self-image 'problem' feel like they are lower down the ladder than they want to be. They think that if only they could climb higher everything would be OK.

But here is the crucial point: the issue is that of being on the ladder in the first place, not how far up we think we are. The question we have to wrestle with is *how* we should define and think about ourselves, not whether we happen to feel OK. The question is where our identity should come from and what that identity truly is.

So we must say that even for the mythical 'well-adjusted' person there are still questions about identity to be answered. And there are usually insecurities about identity below the surface, in many cases fuelling the pride and confidence that everyone else sees. In this sense the person with an obviously low self-image is only the tip of the iceberg – the obvious part of a much larger issue that affects us all.

Identity coming to the surface

Ask yourself a question: how concerned are you about other people's opinion of you? How does this show itself in the time you give to your appearance, or how competently you come across? How does it show itself in your desire for a position or role that it is considered important or successful?

Or turn that idea around and think about how we don't like to be looked down on or thought of negatively by others. Think about how we hide parts of ourselves from one another for fear of what people will think – ultimately whether or not they will accept us.

Put this way, I don't know anyone for whom this is not an issue in some form or other. Ed Welch puts this wonderfully well, referring to it as the 'fear of man'. He says, 'Fear of man is such a part of our human fabric that we should check for a pulse if someone denies it'!

Coming to the surface of the Christian life

This concern for the acceptance and affirmation of others can show itself in some very practical areas of the Christian life. (If you are not a Christian you may want to skip this section – just jump on to the next heading below.) I think of what I call the 'service test' and the 'evangelism test'.

The service test is whether I am prepared to serve people as Jesus did – that is *really* serve them, rather than serve them just as long as they know they should think well of me because of my great service! As long as my service is gaining me something in the eyes of others, I'm happy to serve, but if my service means I'm viewed as a servant and treated like a servant, then suddenly I'm not so keen. I want people to think well of me and place me at the top of the Christian ladder, not the bottom!

The evangelism test is how I worry about people's opinion of me when I speak about Jesus. I will speak readily if people are interested and think I'm a source of knowledge, but will quickly fall silent when I see that their view of me is taking a down turn. I'm actually very worried about what they will think of me and concerned to show I'm not weird. And that concern is not simply about making sure they have a good view of Jesus, I want them to have a good view of me!

When we are honest about this, it is shocking. The fact is, I can spend more time thinking about what people thought of my clever contribution to the Bible study than about whether that contribution helped anyone. I can worry over the impression my new item of clothing or sporting achievement made on my non-Christian friends more than I worry over an opportunity to speak to them about Jesus.

I can easily be more concerned over my perceived image than I am about sin in my life. I can day-dream endlessly about a greater image for me and fail to consider God. This influences all my relationships and all my motivations within those relationships. And so it is a massive challenge to godliness and serving Jesus. Often it means we don't do the right thing, or we do the right thing but for the wrong motive.

Robert Murray M'Cheyne was a Scottish church minister in the nineteenth century. He knew of the temptation to live life aware of everyone else's opinion, and how this changed the way he lived for God. He was considering going into missionary work and said:

> If I am to go to the heathen to speak of the unsearchable riches of Christ, this one thing must be given me, to be out of the reach of the baneful influence of esteem or contempt.

Here's a man who knows his heart well enough to be honest about this. He knows he needs God to help him be free of the influence of other people's opinions, whether it's esteem or contempt. One main aim of this book is to answer that prayer; to help us be out of reach of what M'Cheyne calls that 'baneful influence'.

The life on show

Someone once commented to me, 'I feel my life is a performance sometimes.' Do you ever feel like that? If you do, I'm not surprised. We've been saying that we are concerned about our image before other people – how others view us. That means we live looking to them for an evaluation: our life is on show and we are worried about what the audience thinks of the performance.

At its worst, this means that life is effectively run by other people. Friends, family, work colleagues, church community and neighbours become all-determining in how we live. Life feels like a variety of roles played out in front of different audiences where the aim of the game is to get applause from them all.

Sally made the comparison between everyday life and an interview. She said, 'I want to be liked and accepted – like in an interview situation where you read the signs and try to be what they want.' She puts it well – we want to be what other people want us to be.

Life like that means we don't really know who we are. Life like that actually makes it hard to relate well to other people – they're viewed as a potential source of comfort and reassurance or a potential threat, especially if they are similar to us. It turns relationships into a constant source of comparisons. It is a continual weighing up as to where we are on the various ladders of success. It is life lived in a perpetual low-grade identity crisis – which may of course boil up into a full-scale identity crisis given the right circumstances.

I see this in my self-glorifying day-dreams. Some day-dreams of course are harmless enough: I imagine I'm a great singer, speaker, writer, footballer or whatever, and it can be just a bit of fun. However, all too often my day-dreams have me not just being good at something and enjoying it, but *being seen* to be good at something. And then they have me feeling better about myself because I've *been seen* to be so good at it. And behind such day-dreams is the assumption that if only people would see me and think about me like that, then life would be better. At which point I've given the game away. It shows me that I am not secure in myself and so feel the need to project an image.

Identity and Christians

You may not consider yourself a Christian, but you are interested in the question of identity. I want to humbly say that I think the Bible has the answers you are looking for. For the rest of the book, I will be assuming that readers believe in Jesus. In other words I'm writing from the standpoint of being a Christian and for Christians. But please read on. There will be assumptions I make which you may not agree with, but keep going, asking yourself, 'What if this is true?'

If you are a Christian, you should want to know God's mind on this topic and to think in line with it. However there hasn't been a lot of Christian thinking on this topic, and what has been said and written varies greatly. Christian opinion on this has swung into two very different camps.

There are those who say that Christians know they are sinful – rebellious against God – and so they have every reason to think badly of themselves. In fact they *ought* to think badly of themselves. And so every Christian should have a low self-image: it is a mark of godliness!

The other camp emphasizes the reasons why a Christian should have a high self-image. Just think, they say, you are made in God's image and, even though you're a sinner, God loves you so much he sent Jesus to die for you. So you must be worth a lot! And now you're adopted into God's family and an heir of eternal life. You have every reason to hold your head up. A high self-image is the right of every Christian, so they should celebrate!

So here's the issue: Who am I? What is my identity? How should I think of myself?

Looking in the mirror

It's probably about time to explain the title of this chapter. Our identity or self-image is a bit like looking in a mirror, seeing our reflection and making a judgment about ourselves. However, as we've been exploring, the 'mirror' we tend to use is the world around us: how do I compare to others, or what do they think of me? The world around reflects back my image and tells me how I should think of myself.

However there is another mirror we can use. It's the mirror we *should* use! We are told in James 1:23–24 that the word of God, the Bible, is like a mirror. We look into it and we see what we are really like. Here is a description of ourselves that comes, not from our culture, or from within us, but from God. That is the identity we should want to have.

You see, people talk about our self-image being high or low, and it's assumed that a low self-image is a bad thing and a high self-image is a good thing. And they assume we should help those who think badly of themselves to change by thinking better of themselves. *It's crucial for us to get clear from the start that this isn't the issue.*

The key thing is not getting a high self-image but getting a *right* self-image: understanding our identity correctly. We should want to know how God thinks of us, and think of ourselves accordingly. We must listen to him to know our true identity, which is independent of the mirrors of the world.

The famous reformer of the sixteenth century, John Calvin, wrote about this. He was arguing that people always tend to think more of themselves than they should and wanted them to accept how the Bible describes them. Here are his words:

> I require only that, laying aside the disease of self-love and
> ambition, under the blinding influences of which he thinks more
> highly of himself than he ought, he may see himself as he really
> is by looking into the faithful mirror of Scripture.

That's our aim – to lay aside what we might like to be true, and see ourselves as we really are. And the only way to do it is to look into the mirror of the Bible. As you read on, I want to ask you to try to do that: put aside what answers you'd like to get and prepare simply to hear God's voice on the matter.

The majority of us want to hear something flattering about ourselves – so resolve now to hear what God wants to say, not what you'd like to hear. Others of us only expect to hear something negative about ourselves – so resolve to hear what God actually says, not what you expect him to say.

You will also need to be prepared to do some thinking as well. I'll tell you now that this issue is much more complex than either simply thinking well of ourselves or being down on ourselves. God will have some hard truths for us to come to terms with, but also some amazingly wonderful truths about who we are in Christ. And we're going to have to think carefully to put it all together.

You'll also need to be ready to have an honest look at yourself. This is a very personal issue that runs deep within us. It can feel frightening to be honest about it. As a result we can discuss it but want to keep it at arm's length. There will be things to admit about yourself and things to accept from God and it won't always be easy.

But can I also say that it is worth the journey. The person with a clear biblical view of themselves is someone who truly knows who they are. They know what God says about them and how God says they should think of themselves. And so they can sit loose to other people's opinions of them. They know how to respond to their various successes and failures in life without their self-image going up and down like a yo-yo. They can have a sort of self-forgetfulness rather than self-preoccupation. They can consider how to love and serve others rather than impress them. They are at peace with themselves – because they are at peace with God.

Please don't think I'm describing myself there! I'm still working at this, and even as I write I am aware of my failures. My great desire though, is to help us understand the biblical teaching so that, wherever we are at right now, we can all grow towards knowing how God thinks of us and how he wants us to think of ourselves.

So let's look in the mirror.

Questions for reflection or discussion

1. Why is our culture so concerned with feeling good about ourselves?
2. Where do you hear and see messages about self-image around you? How do you react to them?
3. Why is this such a painful issue for many people?
4. How does a concern for image show itself in your life?
5. 'The key thing is not getting a high self-image but getting a right self-image.' What do you think of this idea?
6. How do you feel about reading God's word, and preparing to hear what he says about your identity?

2. Taking the lid off

In a seminar on self-image, Jo wrote down how she tended to think about herself and drew a diagram to illustrate. This is what she said and drew:

> I tend to place myself on a scale from positive to negative in various areas. For example I create a subconscious 'attractiveness' scale and place myself on it. This is then influenced by others, i.e. walking past an attractive person will slide my marker a little lower down; receiving a compliment will nudge the marker up a bit.

Very unattractive –
no one would find
me attractive

Really hot –
I'll turn heads

Jo has captured something about how self-image works. You may not be as bothered about 'attractiveness' but insert 'success at work', 'being thought cool or funny', 'good at sport', or whatever it is for you. We all tend to operate with these sorts of scales.

In the previous chapter we introduced a number of ideas about self-image or identity. In this chapter, we are going to examine how this works more closely. There's nothing especially biblical about this bit but it's useful to take the lid off how we work and take a look inside. Having seen more clearly how we tend to function will then help us in applying biblical truth.

I'm going to use the self-image language a great deal in this chapter. If this language doesn't appeal to you, remember that it is simply about how any one of us defines our identity, how we think about who we are.

Building a self-image

I'd like you to follow a little exercise. Write down or think of a few words to describe yourself. It could be describing your personality, your character, your strengths or weaknesses, your physical features, or your background. Anything that is part of what makes you who you are.

What you are describing in those words is how you think of yourself. It is part of your mental picture of 'you'. That picture is purely descriptive, it doesn't evaluate anything. It is simply looking in the mirror and describing what you see.

What I'd like you to do now is to take that element of yourself that you have described and evaluate it. Write down or decide in your mind what you think about it: is it good or bad, right or wrong, do you like or hate it? Are you not bothered about it or do you want to change it?

What you have written down or thought about this time is the basis for your self-image. While the picture you have of yourself is descriptive, this is now evaluative: it is how we rate our description of ourselves. This is not just how we see ourselves but what we think and feel about what we see.

We can put it together in a simple equation:

Picture of ourselves + evaluation = self-image

So self-image or self-esteem has been defined as:

> . . . the evaluation that a person makes of himself in comparison to some standard, or the way he has come to think about himself habitually.

I should probably mention that self-esteem is actually the more accurate term to use for this. However, when people talk about self-image they usually mean the same thing, and because it's the more common term I'm going to use it.

Our tendency to build our self-image in this way means that there are several issues we need to be aware of. First, there is how we come to think of ourselves in the first place, how we form that picture of ourselves and how accurate that picture is. Second, there are the evaluations we make, the criteria we use in those evaluations and which areas we consider important. Third, there's the influence of our context, which will massively affect this whole process. We're going to think these through in a bit more detail.

Components of self-image

The areas where we might evaluate ourselves to assess our self-image are commonly listed as falling into the four big categories I've described below. As you read through them, think about which areas are particularly important to you.

Your performance of roles

This is how successful you are at what you do. That might be general areas like education, sport, career, home life, or parenting. Or it might be very specific roles – leading a small group Bible study at university, or how good your cooking is. This tells us something about our abilities and how good we are at stuff.

Your 'pedigree'
It makes you sound like a dog, I know, but what is meant is your background, where you are from, your family heritage or status, which school or university you attended, which football team you support. This tells us something about our identity and gives us a source of belonging or pride.

Your acceptability to others
This is how we feel about relationships with our friends, partner or parents. It tells us about our lovability or acceptability to others. This is an area where our background can have a very real effect on the present – our experiences of being loved in the past often flow over into how we view ourselves or evaluate the love of others now.

Your significance
This is the big question of how you think of your significance in the world: where you fit into the grand scheme of things, how you will be remembered, or the impact you will make. These tell us about the meaning our life has.

These are just four broad categories. We can break them down into smaller components. For example, when I ran some seminars on this, I asked people to list the main areas they drew their self-image from. The most common areas were appearance, success at work and status. And to find out about each of those, we looked to other people's opinions.

That was the mirror we all looked in. The picture below illustrates how these factors work in developing our self-image.

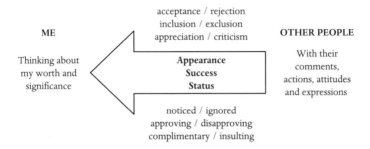

Variations in self-image

Now we must see that we will each approach building our self-image slightly differently. It will vary in a number of ways that we need to explore.

Variations in what we think is important

John is a student. He is worried about his relationships and being thought well of in his college. And so he persistently evaluates himself on whether he has a girlfriend, who she is, what she says about him, and his image among his peers. He also plays football and is good enough to be in the university second team. He would love to be in the first team but is also fearful of being dropped from the seconds. He doesn't really care about success in his studies, and isn't bothered about his background.

Mary is from the north of England and proud of it. She is loud and everyone knows it and likes her for it. She is genuinely unconcerned about her body image or boyfriends but is desperate to be regarded as a 'life and soul of the party' person by her friends. She feels threatened by anyone who may be considered funnier than her. She enjoys music and clubbing and is keen to be seen to be up on the latest releases.

Simon takes his career seriously. He's just been promoted and is feeling good about life. He's not too bothered about relationships at present, apart from the one with his father, and he is keen to impress him with his work success.

Janet is a housewife and mother of two. She is very concerned to be, and appear to be, a competent parent. As a result, she is constantly comparing her children's progress with that of her peers. It's also important to her that her house is considered well presented and she is keen to hear positive comments from visitors about her decorative skills.

Of course we could keep going with descriptions of people. Different things will be important to us depending on our background, our interests and the opportunities life presents us with. As a result some of us will focus on our achievements, while others will only be concerned about how we are loved by others. Probably for most people there is a mix of the issues listed above but they are weighted differently from one person to another.

Just take a moment to think: which are the important areas for you? What do you like to hear people say about you? Which would you feel worst about if you didn't get any positive feedback in that area?

Variations over time

It should take only a moment to realize that our feelings on these subjects can vary enormously from one moment to another. Consider the different feelings you have about yourself when you've just been promoted at work compared to when you've just been disciplined. Or when you're laughing with friends compared to when you are being laughed at. Or when someone said, 'I love you', compared to when they said, 'Let's just be friends'.

So for all of us, self-image will change with our experience of life. However some people tend to have more a stable baseline than others. Mike, for example, when asked how he tended to think of himself, simply said, 'Average. Not brilliant, but not useless, either.' He had a fairly stable view of himself.

On the other hand, Stuart said, 'Sometimes I'm on top of the world as I'm the best. At other times nothing I do can ever meet my high expectations.' He will tend to think of himself in line with his experience of the week, the day, or the hour! The result is that his self-image is very unstable and he rides an emotional roller coaster, all depending on what someone has said or what he has achieved today.

Take a moment to think through how your self-image varies over time. Would you say you have a stable or unstable self-image? How much does your view of yourself vary with the day-to-day feedback you receive?

Variations between situations

When my wife and I moved to live on the campus of a theological college, we soon discovered that all the women who lived nearby baked their own bread. Charis, my wife, had never baked bread in her life, nor had she ever had any friends who thought this was important. But now, surrounded by people who appeared to value home baking, she began to question whether she was a good wife because she didn't bake bread!

For the first (and in fact the only) time in our married life, she began to consider baking. She never actually got round to it – in fact she paid one of the neighbours to supply us with freshly baked bread! We ended up laughing about it, but it is a clear illustration of how different settings can influence us.

This means we can think differently about ourselves between work and home, or between the sports club and the

hall of residence we live in. Or it might be between being with
our old school friends, as opposed to our church friends, and
so on. We instinctively pick up the values and concerns of
those around us, and while we don't change from one setting
to another, the evaluation we make of ourselves can do.

Do you feel better about yourself with one set of people
than another? Chances are your feelings here reveal something about how we assess ourselves differently in different
settings.

Variation in the conclusions we draw

We will also vary in how we think about failure or success.
Let's take the relatively trivial case of being dropped from the
university football first team (but substitute whatever 'failure'
might be important to you).

Some of us will blame something outside ourselves – I got
dropped from the first team because the coach is biased.
Other will blame themselves – I got dropped because I didn't
train hard enough.

Some of us will generalize from the one event to the rest
of life. I got dropped from the first team so I'll never succeed
at anything or because that sort of thing always happens to
me. Others of us will keep events separate: I got dropped but
that doesn't mean anything for my career or friendships.

Some of us will move from specific weaknesses to global
conclusions – I got dropped from the first team so I'm
rubbish. Others will be very specific – I got dropped because
I'm not good enough at football.

And we could then replay all of these scenarios for the
'success' of being promoted to the first team. Again it might
be worth considering your own ways of thinking here. How
do you respond to the successes or failures of life? What conclusions do you draw when you are complimented or put

down? Do you blame or congratulate yourself? Do you generalize to the rest of life?

Mirrors and glasses

An extended illustration might help sum up where we've got to. We've thought about looking in the mirror and evaluating what we see. However the mirror we look in is actually dependent on our setting – different settings reflect back different images. With one group of people it doesn't occur to me to think about how trendy my clothes are, but with another group it's at the front of my mind. In some situations, I'm very aware of my academic ability but not my relationships, but in another setting those two are reversed.

So it is a little like walking round those halls of weirdly shaped mirrors that distort your body. Standing in front of one, you appear tall and thin, but then in front of the next you appear short and fat. They distort your reflection so you don't see yourself as you truly are. They may be flattering or unflattering. Similarly, as we walk around life the world around us sends back its reflection and tells us what to think about ourselves. But it is a distorted picture! It doesn't tell us what we are really like and it varies from one setting to another.

We can then add to the illustration. We've said that we vary in how we evaluate our reflection: we vary in which bit of it is important to us and what conclusions we draw from it. And so it is as if we also wear different glasses that influence what we see. Some may be rose-tinted and so always filter out anything bad or explain it away. I'm not sure what the opposite of rose-tinted glasses is, but others of us may always focus on the negatives and even magnify them.

All of which is to repeat what we said at the end of the last chapter. What we desperately need and what we should desperately want is a clear mirror to look in and have our glasses removed. The only such mirror is God's word. This is where he describes us as we really are and tells us how we should think about ourselves. And the only way to take off our own glasses is to be prepared to read the Bible, listening carefully to whatever God says about us, and to ask for his help by the Holy Spirit to hear and so see ourselves clearly.

I don't mean to suggest it's going to be easy. We tend to have very ingrained ways of thinking which makes this a hard process. It will take time for God's truth of who we are to sink in. It will take time to free ourselves of old patterns of thoughts, and think differently about who we are. But this is time worth taking.

Background issues

In the stereotypical psychiatry session, you lie back on a couch, and the psychiatrist, who usually has a strong German accent, says, 'Tell me about your childhood.' The reason for the question is that our upbringing and early years are very influential on the rest of life, especially if they were negative. That background can often influence this whole area of self-image and how we evaluate ourselves – the glasses each of us tend to wear.

For example if someone was brought up receiving repeated criticism, they can easily think badly of themselves and always assume the worst of other people's opinions. Or if someone was brought up with very strict standards and experienced rejection if those standards weren't met, they can be focused on meeting other people's expectations and their self-image focuses on that more than anything else.

Lucy said of her general way of evaluating herself, 'I tend to think negatively about myself. I look at what I've achieved and the bad things stand out.' That had come from an upbringing where failures were consistently pointed out and criticized and successes were never celebrated. The worst-case scenarios involve abuse (verbal, psychological or physical), abandonment or traumatizing experiences.

Given the Bible's teaching on how we are made, we shouldn't be surprised at this effect. We are made to live in loving relationships with one another, but with our rebellion against God that part of his original design became warped. We now hurt one another as much as we love each other. And that hurt leaves its mark. We'll think a little more about that in our next chapter.

This book isn't going to address some of the issues involved in how your background influences you – for example if you have experienced sexual abuse. If your background involves something that still casts a shadow over you, I would still encourage you to read on because I hope the following chapters will help orientate you to the issues involved in developing a biblical identity. But I would also encourage you to seek counselling from someone with appropriate training.

But for all of us, it is worth considering how my background has affected me. Are there patterns in how I respond in thinking about myself? Are there areas I am worried about, or responses to success or failure, that stem from my upbringing? They will vary from very mild to very major, but they will be there.

The good news is that we are not purely victims. Just because my background has affected me in one way does not mean I have to continue to be trapped in that way of thinking for the rest of my life. Change can happen. And we have to say we are responsible for how we now live: we have choices to make and can't simply blame our past for our present behaviour. Change is possible, and God calls us to change.

Which way forward?

There are a variety of voices that will tell us how we should think about self-image, and especially what we should do if our self-image is low. We'll think briefly about those on offer and evaluate some problems with them before pointing to the route we'll take in the remainder of this book.

Deceive yourself

We are often told that to have a high self-image we must not listen to anything negative about ourselves. We may feel shame and guilt but we will be told that these are false or someone else is to blame. We may feel unloved by others but we will be told that is other people's problem because we are intrinsically lovable.

Here's one example of this approach to improving our self-image:

> Start each day with a self-affirming statement: 'I'm hot, I'm smart, and I'm ready for anything', or 'I'm confident, competent, and full of energy'. Give yourself compliments that pump up your sense of power.

This 'just believe in yourself' approach involves deceiving yourself. The fact is, we may not be 'hot, smart and ready for anything'. The fact is, we may fail and it may indeed be our fault.

The model and actress Joanna Lumley admitted that she tore up reviews about her that said anything negative. She did so because, for her, they would then not exist. We may not have reviews written about us, but we will be told to do the same thing to anything that casts us in a bad light – just ignore it, pretend it doesn't exist.

This approach also tells us not to listen to our own criticism or self-doubts because we might discover we're not

the person we thought we were and want to be. The singer
Robbie Williams gives an example of this approach. He
said:

> Do you know how I get through being self critical? Never listen
> to it, ever. If I listen to it, perhaps my deepest, darkest fears will
> be proved right, and then I wouldn't get onstage again.

This approach calls us to live in our own fantasy world where
we only believe what we tell ourselves. And so any high self-
image that is created is fragile and delicate. A small dose of
reality can bring it crumbling to the ground.

Reinvent yourself

One of the great cries of our culture – especially to those who
are younger – is that we can be 'whatever we want to be'. It's
voiced on TV reality shows and competitions. It's echoed in
magazines and lived out in films. If only we believe in ourselves and give ourselves to our dreams, we will achieve
them. I saw an example in a self-help type book this week. It
boldly stated, 'Everything you don't like about yourself can
be improved.'

Of course there's nothing wrong with ambition and hopes
in themselves. What's wrong is the assumption that if you
don't like yourself very much, you can become the person
you want to be. You can reinvent yourself through changes
of career, relationship, car, housing, hairstyle or diet.

While there's nothing wrong with a change in direction in
life for the right reasons, this approach is kidding ourselves
that we can escape who we are and become someone new. In
the new clothes, with the new hairstyle, driving the new car
and even in the new career, it's still the same me with the same
questions, same fears, same doubts and same problems. I may

feel a little different but in reality all I've done is managed to put off the question of my self-image a little longer.

Understand yourself

A common approach is to try to understand better how we create our own self-identity. For example it might reveal to someone that they always focus on the things they do poorly rather than well, and this has led to a low self-image. They would then be helped to explore why that is, perhaps discovering that it comes from assumptions they've held from childhood.

Or someone might discover that they always generalize their experiences in a way that reflects badly on them. For example, they think someone was rude to them because they are insignificant, rather than because the person was in a bad mood. Or they say photos of them are unappealing because they are ugly rather than because they're not photogenic. Again they would then be helped to explore why they generalize in that way and to change the well-worn paths their thoughts run in.

This can be very helpful – it takes the lid off our patterns of thinking and gives us a look inside. In many instances it will reveal the influence of our background and may show us where we are illogical in our reactions to people and circumstances.

But there are two fundamental problems with this from a Christian point of view. First it begins with the assumption that I should feel OK about myself, and tries to change my ways of thinking to bring that about. But it cannot actually begin to tell me what I *ought* to think about myself. Secondly, it hopes that understanding myself better will solve any problems – but what if it doesn't? What if I *should* feel down on myself? There is greater understanding here but little hope.

Think badly of yourself

I mentioned in the last chapter that some Christian writers on this topic say we ought to think badly of ourselves. That's something of a simplification but that's the bottom line. This view often focuses on our sinfulness and says that we ought to despise ourselves rather than seek to feel good about ourselves.

A favourite Bible verse that is often picked up here is Jesus' command to deny ourselves and put ourselves to death (Mark 8:34). This is taken to be the opposite of having a high self-image where we affirm ourselves. So one writer says:

> Jesus is saying, 'You must treat yourself, with all your sinful ways, priorities and desires, like a criminal and put yourself to death every day'. That says something about the self-image that Christ expects us to have!

Now we must say that there is truth in this – if we know anything of the Bible's picture of us we should know that it's far from pretty! In chapter four we will look closely at the Bible's teaching on our sinfulness. However I think this view is emphasizing only one strand of biblical teaching and there is far more to the picture than our sinfulness alone.

Think well of yourself

I've also mentioned that some Christian writers think Christians have every reason for a very positive self-image. They go so far as to say that it is sinful to think badly of ourselves or to think that we are worthless.

The recommendation for one such book says the following: 'This book will help thousands to realize that they are the most important person in their lives.' Another writer, having outlined biblical reasons for a positive view of self, says,

'If you're beginning to think you're someone special as a Christian, you're thinking right – you are special.'

Again, there are elements of truth here, but it tends to avoid our sinfulness. Also it seems to make the Bible's teaching about God's love and goodness revolve around me. We'll need to explore this area much more carefully.

Think biblically about yourself!

What we are going to do is survey the biblical teaching on how God has made us, what we have done in sinning against him, and what he has done in saving us. In all this, we will be asking the questions, what is my identity, and how should I think about myself? We need to be aware of the dangers of introspective navel gazing, but my hope and prayer is that we will see ourselves as we should, and so have the image God would want us to have.

Questions for reflection or discussion

1. Do you agree with the model of how we build self-image?
2. Which areas are most important for you in building self-image or defining yourself?
3. What variations do you see in your self-image over time or between different situations?
4. What conclusions do you tend to draw about yourself from your 'successes' or 'failures'?
5. Is there anything in your background that has influenced how you think about yourself or how you react to other people's opinions of you?
6. What is helpful about 'taking the lid off' and seeing how we tend to think in this area?
7. Do you have a tendency to think well of yourself or think badly of yourself? How do you feel about hearing what God has to say?

3. the original design

Who are you? What are you worth? What is your identity?

These are questions people have wrestled with down through the centuries, and there are lots of different answers. We can divide them into a few groups.

We're lucky

There are those who believe that creation is here because of some cosmic chance event and that we all evolved from a primeval swamp. And so we're no different from the rest of the animal kingdom around us; we just happen to have evolved a few stages further on than everything else.

If you say that, then it's only logical to believe that we're not actually any different from the rest of the animals we see around us. You have to say that we've got no inherent value; or at least no more value than a dolphin or a dog or a dung beetle. Instead we are simply those who are lucky enough to be at the top of the evolutionary tree.

We're gods

At the opposite end of the spectrum, we're not animals at all, no, we're more like gods! We're amazing and should think wonderful thoughts of ourselves. You see this sort of thing when people talk about a divine spark in each of us or about discovering the god within us. Some people take this idea very literally and really think we are all mini-gods. Indeed this forms part of some religions. For others it's a much vaguer idea but it still results in thinking big thoughts of ourselves. You can see it in the adverts that tell us to 'Reveal the goddess inside you', or to 'Discover the hero inside yourself'.

We're what we can offer

Then there's the position where your view of yourself all depends on what you have to offer the world. The scales that are used vary: it might be to do with how useful or productive you are, or it might be how intelligent, beautiful or funny you are. But whatever scale is used, who we are and what we are worth all depends on what we have to offer and how we compare with those around us.

Back to the beginning

What we need to do is go back to the beginning to look at God's original design for us. Only there do we find the foundational truths that tell us who we really are. Here's what we read in the first chapter of the Bible about how God made us:

> Then God said, 'Let us make human beings in our image, in our likeness, so that they may rule over the fish in the sea and the birds in the sky, over the livestock and all the wild animals, and over all the creatures that move along the ground.'
> (Genesis 1:26)

This is key: *we are made in the image of God*. The word 'image' there is like the word 'model'. This becomes clear when we see the other word that goes along with 'image': we are made in God's image and *likeness*. We are made like God; we are like a model based on him.

Begin with God, not us

This means that to know ourselves we have to begin with God. The thing about an image is that it doesn't exist by itself – an image is defined by the one whose image it is. So if we're made in God's image, to know ourselves we must know and understand something about him.

This teaches us something really important that will run through the rest of this book. Our identity comes from beyond ourselves: it is dependent on God and how he's made us (and as we'll see later, how he has saved us). Any search for identity that doesn't begin with God is bound to fail; it's a search that has taken a wrong turn at the very start. John Calvin phrased it well:

> No man can take a survey of himself but he must immediately turn to the contemplation of God in whom he lives and moves; because it is perfectly obvious, that the endowments which we possess cannot possibly be from ourselves.

But all around us people are trying to define who they are, what they are worth, and what their significance is, *on their own*. What happens when we try to do this of course is that we look within or around us for answers. If we look within, we turn to what we feel or think about ourselves. If we look around us, we turn to our relationships with other people, our roles in life, our possessions or our hobbies or whatever else appeals to us, and we try to find our identity in them. And in doing so we ignore the God who made us.

But we're not going to begin *our* search to understand ourselves in that way. We know that our self-image or identity will come from looking to the God who made us. I was talking to Jenny about the source of our identity and she was struck by this point: 'It's not all about me!' she said, 'Looking at myself and getting a right view of who I am means looking to God and who he is. I need to focus on him because by seeking him I can find out who I really am.'

This means we must be humble in our approach. We have to admit that, left to ourselves, we can't discover our identity and solve our self-image problem. We can't discover who we are; we can only be told who we are. We must be taught this by God.

Let me give one example of the difference this makes. It is common in Christian discussions of self-image to be told, 'God loves us so we should feel OK about ourselves', or something similar. Now we are going to see in later chapters that there is something very true about this sort of statement. But we need to see now that there can also be something very wrong with it if it revolves around me and my needs and thinks that God is the solution.

This approach begins with me and defines life on my terms: I want to feel more loved, and because I'm a Christian I look to God to fill that need. God becomes my cosmic counsellor who tells me I'm OK. But that keeps me at the centre. It starts with me and my needs and ends with me and my solution – who happens in this case to be God. But when I realize that my identity comes from God (he made me and so he defines me), then I need to begin with him. I must start with the question, 'Who are you and how have you made me?', not 'What can you give me?'

Image means what?

So what does it means to be made in God's image? In what way are we like God? In the verse above the idea of image was linked with our rule over creation. We're made rulers in the image of God, the supreme ruler. That link between image and rule comes again later in the same chapter in Genesis. Here it is:

> So God created human beings in his own image,
> in the image of God he created them;
> male and female he created them.
>
> God blessed them and said to them, 'Be fruitful and increase in number; fill the earth and subdue it. Rule over the fish in the sea and the birds in the sky and over every living creature that moves on the ground.' (Genesis 1:27–28)

We are made to fill the earth and subdue it. That means to bring it under control. And God says again we are to rule over it. We're put in charge of creation.

This rule of the world is on God's behalf. He is the supreme ruler and we're simply his image bearers. We're like his appointed guardians who rule for him. And so we should rule creation knowing we live under his rule ourselves, loving and obeying him as our God whose image we have been given.

Notice also that being made in God's image refers to people as a whole, a community: people who are created as both male and female and who multiply in number. So our rule over creation isn't simply about each of us as individuals. It's about us ruling as a community where we relate to one another. In this way, we also reflect God's image as he rules as a loving community of three people: Father, Son and Spirit. We should reflect that loving community in our relationships with each other.

We can picture all this in a diagram:

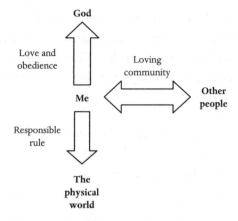

We are made to live in relationship with God, with one another and with our world. I am under God, alongside other people and over the world. I am made to live in love and obedience to God, in loving community with others and as a responsible ruler of creation. To understand our true identity we must understand that three-fold relationship, because that is how God has made me.

Living in the real world

Sometimes I hear people say that a Christian's self-image should come only from their relationship with God. Their view of themselves should be independent of everything else in life. It's as if nothing that happens matters to me because I'm secure in God.

I know what people mean by that, but I disagree. And the reason why I disagree is because of this point: the way God has made us involves not only our relationship with him but also living alongside other people and over the world. So I should *expect* to be affected by my relationships with other people, and I should *expect* to be affected by my role and work in the world. These things are part of how I've been made.

Take the example of other people: because I'm made to live in relationship with people, things like loneliness or isolation are very real and will affect me. Things like other people's rejection of me will hurt. God made us to live in loving community with other people and so I will be affected by my relationships.

Take the example of our role in the world – being made to be a ruler of the world means that I work in the world in a productive way. But that can now go wrong: I can be unemployed or unable to work; I can be in a mind-numbingly boring job, or an exceptionally burnt-out stressful job. And this too will affect me. I can't become immune to my role and experience of work – that too wouldn't be living in the real world.

I will be affected by my friendships, my parents, my health, my skills, my career success or failure, my surroundings, my hobbies and everything else. To deny this is to deny how God has made us.

The question is how all these things affect me. That's something we'll return to later in this book.

Humble dignity

Being made in the image of God has great implications for how we think of ourselves. I want to sum it up with the phrase 'humble dignity'. I'll warn you now, this is the catch phrase for the rest of the book. It's my attempt to sum up how we should feel about ourselves given a biblical self-image. So say it to yourself and get used to the sound of it! Humble dignity.

Our humble dignity starts with creation in God's image. Let me explain:

We're only an image . . .

We must remember that while we are made in the image of God, we are only an image. And an image is not the thing itself. So we are not gods ourselves and we must beware of thinking that we are. We mustn't think more of ourselves than we should – we should remind ourselves that we are only an image.

Along with this, we must remember that this status, in fact our whole being and identity, is *derived* from God. We are made like this only because he chose to make us like this. Imagine telling someone they are made in the image of God and they respond by saying, 'Well done me!' That would be both weird and wrong. You can't pat yourself on the back for this – it would be like saying well done to yourself for where you were born. This is something we are humble about because it is a gift that God has given to us.

And we must also remember that we remain dependent on him as his image. He gives us every breath we breathe; he holds us together; it is only by his will we exist. Paul says that it is only in God 'we live and move and have our being' (Acts 17:28). We do not and we cannot stand by ourselves. Rather we stand infinitely below our Creator, utterly dependent on him. And for all these reasons there should be great humility.

. . . but the image of God

But we must also remember that we are made in the image of the glorious Creator himself! This is our privilege alone as humans. God makes an amazing world in Genesis 1, but only humanity is made in his image. This is what gives us value and status in his creation.

So one theologian writes, 'Mankind is in the image of God and he alone; this singular honour marks him out as God's choice creature.' Having reminded ourselves of the need for humility, we must also remind ourselves of our great dignity.

This is an incredible position to be given: a position of value and respect. Talking to two people about being made in the image of God, John simply said, 'Awesome!' while Amanda spoke of the sense of privilege it gave her. That's right – it is awesome and it is a huge privilege.

It has been said that this truth – being made in God's image – should lift the head of the poorest beggar *and* bend the knee of the most exalted king. I think that's right: it both gives us great dignity and keeps us humble before God.

The value we have

Just imagine if someone took a photo of you and then ripped it up in front of you. How would you feel? Worried? Angry? You'd feel something because ripping up that photo wasn't simply destroying a piece of paper and ink, it was destroying a representation of you.

It's not a perfect analogy, but we are a little like photos of God, representations of him bearing his image. We are of course much more than photographs, but the point is that our value is related to God. We're valuable because we bear his image just like that photo was valuable because it bore your image.

We see this in Genesis 9 where God says how wrong it would be to kill another person. This is what he says:

Whoever sheds human blood,
  by human beings shall their blood be shed;
for in the image of God
  has God made humanity. (Genesis 9:6)

This is why it is OK to kill animals but not to kill people – we are made in God's image and they are not. There is a value to people because of how God has made us.

And so we see the great dignity people have, such that they should be treated with respect. But it is always related to God – they have value because of their relationship with him, and so do we. Once again this isn't something we can take pride in, or even demand as 'our' right. It is something we thank God for.

When I think about it, it's amazing!
Just get the feel of that humble dignity in Psalm 8:

> When I consider your heavens,
>   the work of your fingers,
> the moon and the stars,
>   which you have set in place,
> what are mere mortals that you are mindful of them,
>   human beings that you care for them?
> You have made them a little lower than the heavenly beings
>   and crowned them with glory and honour.
> You made them rulers over the works of your hands;
>   you put everything under their feet:
> all flocks and herds,
>   and the animals of the wild,
> the birds in the sky,
>   and the fish in the sea,
>   all that swim the paths of the seas.
> LORD, our Lord,
>   how majestic is your name in all the earth! (Psalm 8:3–9)

This psalm is a reflection on Genesis 1 on being made in God's image. But this isn't dry theological reflection, this is praise to God for giving us such an exalted position. Do you see what he says? We've been made rulers, we've been crowned with glory and honour! Do you hear the sense of wonder in it? It's as if the writer just can't quite believe it. When he thinks about creation, he asks himself – who am I that you should care for us like this and give us this incredible status?

And yet this exalted position isn't made to be something that revolves around me; it doesn't tell me how great I am, but how generous and caring God is. This isn't a reason for pride, but a reason for praise. We truly have been crowned with glory and honour, and yet only because God chose to crown us in this way. And so we should revel in who we are, but we should do so remembering how good God is for making us like this.

Read through the psalm again and praise God for how he has made us. Say to yourself, 'Who I am that God made me like this? And yet he did! He crowned *me* with glory and honour.' And finish by saying, 'How majestic is *your* name in all the earth!'

True for everyone

What do you need to qualify for this humble dignity in creation? You simply need to be a person! This is true for everyone. So here we have the beginnings of a self-image that is independent of all the other stuff that usually comes into play. Just think about the judgments that are made on people's worth based on how physically attractive, how able-bodied, how intelligent, how old or young they are, or the colour of their skin, or any other scale that's used. All of this falls flat in the light of the truth that our identity is determined *only* by the fact of creation in God's image – and that is true of all people.

We're going to have to let this sink in. You probably knew about being made in God's image before you started reading this chapter. But now you'll need to take this on board for how you view yourself. You'll need to start to make this part of your identity. Here are a few reflections from other people that might help:

- 'I feel a little shallow for not having thought about this before, and a bit self-obsessed to have left God out of the self-image equation.'
- 'This makes me feel I'm not actually as rubbish as I sometimes think I am.'
- 'I need to remember the specialness of being in God's image.'
- 'I should feel more amazed at this. I tend to compare myself to others rather than realizing what God thinks of me in making me in his image.'
- 'This makes my outward appearance and flaws less important, as we have been wonderfully made.'
- 'I'm overwhelmed that God would bother with me or humanity at all – let alone to bestow us with something of himself.'
- 'I feel a sense of undeservedness. And wonder.'

Looking in the mirror

So when I come to look in the mirror of God's word I am told that I have great dignity, humble dignity, but dignity nonetheless. And so no matter what else is true of me, or what has happened to me that day or that week, I should remind myself of my identity as made in God's image.

Along with this humble dignity, as I look in the mirror of God's word I discover that he created me to rule his world, together with other people. He made me to relate to those around me in loving community, and to relate to him as my Creator and my Lord. And so we must say more about this humble dignity than simply that we have it as an individual possession. We have it in the context of living with God as our God, whose image we possess, and living with other people as family and living in this creation. That means that my identity must never be thought of as something I sit back and enjoy, but rather something I live out. We'll return to this idea in a later chapter.

Questions for reflection or discussion

1. Some people define themselves as being (a) lucky, (b) gods, or (c) by what they can offer. Which of these do you think is most common? What results does that have in how we tend to think of ourselves?

2. Why is it so important to start with God and how he has made us in defining who we are?

3. What is so significant about being made in the image of God?

4. What are you struck by in how God has made you to relate to him, other people or the world around you?

5. What do you think of the concept of 'humble dignity'? How is this different from how you may have thought of yourself?

6. Psalm 8 praises God for our dignity as a gift from him. Which phrases or ideas from that psalm do you most need to take on board?

4. the shameful admission

This chapter comes with a warning label. The accepted mantra of our culture is that we mustn't do ourselves down, but build ourselves up. We mustn't look for reasons to think badly of ourselves, but for more and better reasons to admire ourselves. Above all, we're told that we need to love and accept ourselves the way we are.

But for the Christian there is the small matter of being a sinner.

As we look in the mirror of God's word, to know ourselves as we truly are, we will see that we are sinful. Within our self-image or identity there needs to be a clear recognition of that sinfulness. And not just the fact of it, which is often mentioned, but the awfulness of it. It is awful both in what it is, and in what it produces, and there is no other response to this sinfulness than deep shame.

Now whatever you do please don't stop reading either now or at the end of this chapter. We are going step by step and there are more steps to come. So if your heart sinks as you read this chapter (as it should), press on, because this certainly isn't the end of the story.

The awful nature of sin

Satan's words in Genesis 3 show us the heart of sin. He said, 'God knows that when you eat of it your eyes will be opened, and you will be like God' (Genesis 3:5). The temptation to Adam and Eve was that they would themselves become like God. That's what they wanted and that's what we want. Not to have to live under the authority of someone else, but to be top dog.

The picture Jesus paints is that we try to kill God. He tells the story of tenants left in charge of a vineyard who don't want to pay their dues to the owner. And so, when the owner's son comes along, they think to themselves, 'Let's kill him and the inheritance will be ours' (Mark 12:7). They're not happy just being tenants, they want to be owners themselves, and so given the chance they try to kill off God's Son. And so do we.

Do you see that this is a deep-seated rebellion that tries to throw off God as God? As a result, the Bible pulls no punches in the language it uses to describe what we've done: words like evil and wicked. This is a long way away from how we often think about sin today. Too often it is referred to as the mistakes we make, or our selfish choices or our self-destructive behaviour. Rather than naming it for what it is: the crime of history where we have tried to push God off his rightful throne.

Back in the Middle Ages, a church leader called Anselm was involved in a discussion with people who thought it was fairly easy for God to forgive people for their sinfulness. 'He can just forgive us if he wants to,' they said. 'What's the big deal?' Anselm replied, 'You have not yet considered the gravity of sin.' His words could be applied to us today – we have watered down sin so that it is a light thing, and we haven't considered its gravity.

The awful results of sin

The Bible is then very clear about the appalling consequences of this rebellion. Paul puts together a series of quotes on the topic in Romans 3:10–18. It's not pleasant reading:

> As it is written:
> 'There is no one righteous, not even one;
>   there is no one who understands;
>   there is no one who seeks God.
> All have turned away,
>   they have together become worthless;
> there is no one who does good,
>   not even one.'
> 'Their throats are open graves;
>   their tongues practise deceit.'
> 'The poison of vipers is on their lips.'
> 'Their mouths are full of cursing and bitterness.'
> 'Their feet are swift to shed blood;
>   ruin and misery mark their ways,
> and the way of peace they do not know.'
> 'There is no fear of God before their eyes.'

Just read it through again, putting your own name in the appropriate places. Go on, try it!

Feels uncomfortable, doesn't it? And in case we think this is the exception that might describe some really bad people somewhere, just look at what Paul says in Titus 3:

> At one time we too were foolish, disobedient, deceived and
> enslaved by all kinds of passions and pleasures. We lived in malice
> and envy, being hated and hating one another. (Titus 3:3)

Do you see who he is describing? He uses the word 'we'. He includes himself and all of his Christian readers in this description. And we shouldn't flinch from thinking of ourselves the same way either.

We hear the same things in Jesus' words that tell us that we have bad hearts which are the source of evil in the world:

> What comes out of you is what defiles you. For from within, out of your hearts, come evil thoughts, sexual immorality, theft, murder, adultery, greed, malice, deceit, lewdness, envy, slander, arrogance and folly. All these evils come from inside and defile you. (Mark 7:20–23)

Not a pleasant list, is it? And again, this is what is coming out of your heart and mine.

I remember talking to a student who was coming to grips with his own sinfulness. He'd been realizing that he wasn't actually the nice person he liked to think he was. At one point he looked me in the eye and said in anguish, 'Graham you don't understand. My mind is a sewer.' I still remember the look on his face – a mixture of horror and shame at himself.

Jesus would have looked right back at him and said, 'That's right.' And he would say it to each of us, whether we feel particular shame or not. This is who we are and what we produce. Getting to know myself better will include getting to know how sinful I am.

'Well, I'm not perfect, but . . .'

Compare this to the standard view around today. It usually runs along the lines of, 'Well, I'm not perfect, but I am a nice person.' But according to Jesus, we are so far off perfect it's ridiculous to claim to be close. Or we might say, 'I know I make mistakes, but deep down I'm good.' But according to Jesus, the deeper we go into our hearts the worse it gets.

We think of ourselves as basically good people who are capable of doing some bad things on occasion, whereas Jesus says we are evil people who are still capable of doing some good things. (This is exactly how he describes us in Matthew 7:11: '. . . if you then, though you are evil, know how to give good gifts to your children . . .')

This is an area of Christian belief that we tend to acknowledge, and then quickly move on. It's not a pretty sight, so we don't want to stay to take in the view. Chatting to one student about this, he was honest enough to say it made him feel uncomfortable and he wanted to 'gloss over it' and move on to something more cheerful. I think he speaks for us all.

But we can't gloss over it. We must take it very seriously because the view that we are nice people who should think well of ourselves runs so deeply in our culture. The wrong things we do are blamed on our upbringing, or our early experiences, or something in society around us. But whatever it is, it isn't blamed on our having a bad heart.

Helping people with a low view of themselves is often seen as leading people to regard themselves as 'good' and to think of any shame they feel as inappropriate. And with this insight, they can stop hating and start loving themselves. Such self-love is seen as the route to being more psychologically healthy and balanced.

Jesus wouldn't have made it as a modern-day counsellor, would he? But then again, he was the most loving person who ever lived, and so this is simply the truth we must face up to.

Dangerous territory

You may have started reading this book hoping it would help you feel better about yourself and right now you are wondering about putting it down. You may feel your problem is that you think too negatively about yourself rather than too positively. And so the reassuring strokes of our culture (feel good about yourself) and even the warm words of some Christians (you have to love and accept yourself as you are) are very appealing.

I need to say two things. One is what I mentioned at the start of the chapter – keep reading because the story isn't yet finished! But secondly, I have to say we need to face up not only to our sinfulness but also to our temptation to play it down. We must all realize we are on dangerous territory, because the temptation to think well of ourselves is alive and well within us all.

Psalm 36 speaks about wicked people who don't fear God, but rather make their own estimation of who they are and consequently think well of themselves. Here's the killing line from it:

> In their own eyes they flatter themselves too much to detect or
> hate their sin. (Psalm 36:2)

That could so easily be me – I can flatter myself, and think well of myself so that I actually stop thinking of myself as a sinner. I become unaware of my sin, let alone hating my sin and feeling bad about it.

Remember Jesus' harshest words were for those who tended to think well of themselves and had forgotten the sin inside them, and his warmest words were for those who recognized that sin and were honest about it. And so we should be very wary of those voices that would lead us to think well of ourselves.

Richard Baxter, a very insightful seventeenth-century minister, said this about our tendencies:

. . . man's nature is generally disposed to self-exalting, and pride
and self-love are sins so common and so strong, as that it is a thing
of wondrous difficulty to overcome them.

Robert Murray M'Cheyne wrote the following words:

> I know I have cause to be humble and yet I do not know one half
> of that cause. I know I am proud and yet I do not know the half
> of that pride.

These are writers from a different time to ours and they have
something profound to teach us. There is a refreshing
honesty about how they talk of their sinfulness. They are
especially worried about pride, which they see as a dangerous
tendency towards self-exaltation. That's not the instinct of
our culture today; it would be seen as being too down on
yourself. But looking in the mirror of God's word we see we
have good reason to be.

True and false shame

At this point it is worth distinguishing between different
forms of shame. We've been talking about biblical reasons to
feel ashamed of ourselves because we are rightly guilty
before God. However there is also a shame which comes from
our culture rather than from sin. Shame can be felt over
something that is not in itself wrong. Writer and speaker Dick
Keyes has a list of examples. He says:

> Many people are ashamed of being poor . . . others are
> ashamed of not being a success, and they will exaggerate
> the importance of their jobs. But a different person in a
> different social setting might feel ashamed of being rich. Most
> of us at some time are ashamed of our bodies or part of our

bodies . . . We feel shame for what we say and how we say it
. . . We can be ashamed of love that is unreturned. We can be
ashamed of being dependent on others' care because we are
sick.

This is false shame. It is not shame we feel because we've
done something wrong, but shame that comes because of the
expectations of our culture around us. These feelings come
from our desire to fit in and be accepted (which of course is
an issue in itself) but the point for now is that this is nothing
to do with true guilt.

Unfortunately we can all too easily feel more concerned
over this sort of shame than our sin. I can feel more embarrassed about my fashion failures than my moral failures. Lucy
agrees, 'I certainly feel more concerned about what other
people think than concerned about my sin. I loathe myself
when I feel I've messed up a certain situation rather than over
the sin I keep on committing.'

Similarly Alan made this observation: 'I want to live up to
my and others' expectations of me. It's easier to rate the opinions of those who seem tangible. I often feel like I hide my sin
from myself as so much of my sin comes within my thought
life and can be hidden from others.'

Part of my developing a biblical identity is that I feel bad
about what I ought to feel bad about. I should want to feel
guilt and shame for the right reasons. The bottom line is that
I need to care far more about what God thinks than what
people think.

Biblical reasons for a low self-image
All of this understanding on the appalling nature of sin adds
up to give us solid biblical reasons to have a low self-image.
We will move on shortly to how God removes our sin and

restores us in Christ, but we must dwell on the issue of our sin a moment longer.

There are a few biblical examples that make this point well. Isaiah 6 for example shows us someone coming face to face with God. Isaiah has a vision of God in the temple and, seeing his holiness and majesty, he realizes his guilt before God and cries out:

> 'Woe to me! I am ruined! For I am a man of unclean lips, and I live among a people of unclean lips, and my eyes have seen the King, the LORD Almighty.' (Isaiah 6:5)

When he says he is ruined, he means there is no hope for him and he deserves to be wiped out. The reason is because he has become acutely aware of his uncleanness. There is no thinking positively of ourselves here!

Writer C. S. Lewis once commented on how we would feel if we were in the presence of God:

> The real test of being in the presence of God is that you either forget about yourself altogether, or you see yourself as a small dirty object.

This might seem harsh, but given Isaiah's experience above, I think we have to say that Lewis is right.

The same point can be seen in Luke 18. Here we see the worldly schema turned on its head. It's worth reading this one through:

> To some who were confident of their own righteousness and looked down on everyone else, Jesus told this parable: 'Two men went up to the temple to pray, one a Pharisee and the other a tax collector. The Pharisee stood by himself and prayed: "God, I

thank you that I am not like other people – robbers, evildoers, adulterers – or even like this tax collector. I fast twice a week and give a tenth of all I get."

'But the tax collector stood at a distance. He would not even look up to heaven, but beat his breast and said, "God, have mercy on me, a sinner."

'I tell you that this man, rather than the other, went home justified before God. For all those who exalt themselves will be humbled, and those who humble themselves will be exalted.'
(Luke 18:9–14)

Do you see who Jesus has in mind in telling this story? Luke says that he tells it specifically to those who were 'confident of their own righteousness', people who would say to God, 'Thank you, God, that I'm so good.' Whereas the guy in the story who gets it right is the one who says, 'Sorry, God, that I'm so bad.' He sees that he has no reason to hold his head up high before God but only to hang it in shame.

There are times when we see this truth. Jenny described her sense of sin in the following words: 'It's like I'm carrying around a weight I can no longer ignore, a weight that is dragging me down and keeping me from moving forward, a weight of my own making I am ashamed to have hanging over me but am powerless to lift off.' Similarly Ed said he felt 'ashamed and helpless' over his sin, as he realized it was 'not a matter of cleaning up my act but of being rotten to the core'.

Those, I would suggest, are people who have come to understand sin. In saying such things, though, we will be completely out of kilter with the culture around us. It will attempt to reassure us about ourselves and boost our self-image. Adverts will play to our desire to think ourselves as pleasant, likeable and stylish people. We must respond by saying that there are good reasons to have a very low self-image.

Standing before God

We saw in the last chapter that we began with the wonderful ⌐
humble dignity of being made in the image of God. That
image is now badly distorted in us. We have become what
the theologian and writer Francis Schaeffer called 'glorious ruins'. There is still the mark of glory on us, but we
are a shadow of what we were meant to be. In fact
we are a corruption of what we were meant to be.

Wonderfully though, the value of being made in God's
image is not something that is lost after the fall into sin. For
example we read in the last chapter that people will be held
accountable for killing another person because God has made
such people in his image (Genesis 9:6).

Dick Keyes distinguishes in this area between our worth
and our worthiness:

> Sinful people, unworthy as they are, are not worthless. Because of
> sin, humankind is unworthy of the blessing of God in any form.
> We deserve only judicial punishment for our rebellion against
> God. But this is not to say that we have lost all worth or value.

Now a few readers with sharp eyes and good memories might
be thinking of the quote from Romans 3 earlier that seems to
contradict this. It said that we had together become 'worthless' (Romans 3:12). Well, that word would be better
translated as 'corrupt'; it has the idea of no longer being suit-
able for original use. It's still not a nice word – but it doesn't
mean we are worthless.

However we must distinguish between this inherent value
that we have because of how God made us and any idea of

niceness, worthiness or acceptability. This is where we need to hold things together that we would not usually combine. We are used to someone's value being directly related to something else about them: it is how nice or good they are which means they have value.

Here though, we are told we are evil and wicked and *yet still of value* because of how God made us. This is the value that the criminal still has, despite the awfulness of his crime because he is still made in the image of God. That is how we should think of ourselves – the value we have is the lasting value of how God originally made us.

Standing before other people

When Oliver Cromwell was going to have his portrait painted, he gave the artist the following instruction:

> I desire you would use all your skill to paint my picture truly like me and do not flatter me at all; but remark all the roughness, pimples, warts and everything.

That's where we get the expression 'warts and all' from. We might be happy enough with a true likeness of us in a picture – although most of us would still want the warts airbrushed out. But none of us want the state of our hearts to be seen 'warts and all'. There's too much of us that we want to hide from one another, and even from ourselves.

The pity is that this isn't how God made us to relate to each other. Back in Genesis 2, Adam and Eve were 'naked and felt no shame' (Genesis 2:25). What a wonderful picture of the openness and intimacy they had with each other. But after they rebelled against God, 'the eyes of both of them were opened, and they realized they were naked; so they sewed fig leaves together and made coverings for themselves' (Genesis 3:7).

Here is the start of our shame before other people – our desire not be seen, especially not to be seen 'warts and all'. I now feel shame when other people look at me. It raises the questions, 'What will they think of me?', 'Will they accept me?' This can result in living in fear of being discovered for who we are. We put on masks and play certain roles which deceive others about who we are and what we're like.

There are often three versions of me hanging around. There is the real me as I really am. Then there's the person I'd like to think of myself as. As finally there's the person I'd like everyone else to think I am. There isn't one integrated me that I am happy to live with, and certainly not to present to others. Because of my sin, I don't want to know myself truly, let alone allow others to know me truly.

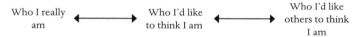

You see the fullest versions of this in the on-line communities, whether in the personal pages and groups on Facebook or in whole-life games like Second Life. In these I can create my on-line version of me – my avatar. I choose how it looks and how I am described. And then I can interact with other people pretty much on my terms. They can only see the bits of me I want them to see. Please don't think I'm against all on-line communication and that we all deliberately deceive each other through it – not at all. But I do think it's very revealing about how we want to present ourselves.

I was talking with a discussion group about how we feel about standing in front of other people. Here are some of the reasons they gave for feeling they needed to project an image:

- 'To gain acceptance from others because I'm insecure about my identity.'

- 'Because if people see the reality of who I am, it makes me vulnerable.'
- 'To try and meet what I see as the expectations people think they see in me, or to show a bigger, better image.'
- 'Because I want to have self-confidence, I want people to have a certain impression of me.'
- 'To gain status and importance; to be accepted, liked and even looked up to.'
- 'I feel people might reject me if they know the "real me".'

This shame before other people leads to distorted relationships. We've said already we hide from each other. We don't want to be seen for who we really are, for fear of being rejected. We see that in people's honest reflections above. Put differently, we feel the need to project a certain image of ourselves that people will like.

But this also means we can quite like discovering other people's faults. We can enjoy the failures of others so that we can reassure ourselves that they are no better than us. Ideally they are worse than us. We can see this on the personal level in our love of gossip that puts others down. We can see it on the national media level in how we love the exposure of the rich and famous.

One of the things we'll go on to think about later is that the Christian community should be free from these distortions. There should be the freedom to be honest about who we really are and the ability to accept and love others rather than want to look down on them.

Looking in the mirror
Having seen the humble dignity that we were given in creation we now need to look in the mirror and make a

shameful admission. We are guilty. We have good reason to feel ashamed. We don't make this admission to feel sorry for ourselves. We don't do it to beat ourselves up. We do this because it is God's diagnosis of our condition – it is facing up to reality. And we need to face it so that we can accept God's remedy.

God doesn't want us to wallow in our guilt and shame, but wipe us clean from it and know how accepted we are. That's what we'll think about in the next chapter. But – and it's a big 'but' – we must have admitted this first. If we haven't, we will never have the security of God's acceptance, because we will keep on thinking it has something to do with how nice or acceptable I am. Once I realize how bad I am, then I can truly realize and embrace how gracious God's acceptance is. That's what we need to think about now.

Questions for reflection or discussion

1. What is it about sin that makes it such a terrible thing?
2. Where do you hear encouragements to play down the gravity of sin? How should you respond?
3. Do you need to view your sinfulness more seriously? If so, in what way?
4. Where are you aware of false shame rather than true shame? How will you respond to this?
5. What effect does your sinfulness have on how you relate to those around you?
6. I've been created in God's image, but have now rebelled and am a sinner. How should I think about myself in light of this?

5. the new beginning

So far we've seen our original identity in creation – the humble dignity of being made in God's image. And then we've seen the horrible nature of our sinful rebellion. You may have finished the last chapter a little depressed – and for good reason. Now though, comes the wonder of God's grace. Be amazed!

The parable of the amazing Father

One of Jesus' best known parables is that of the prodigal son. It comes in Luke 15 where Jesus is trying to convince people about God's heart towards sinners. I don't think the parable is very well named, because it's not really about the son but all about the amazing father.

The son in this story commits the worst of acts. He asks for his inheritance early, which is basically the same as saying that he wishes his father was dead so he can get the money now. Just imagine saying that seriously to your parents! This isn't just being rude, this is wanting independence, wanting to be away from the rule of his father. This is a picture of our sin.

Once he has rejected his father, the son proceeds to waste away all his inheritance in wild living. He ends up impoverished and desperate. Eventually he thinks to himself that his father might allow him to come back home to work as a servant. Here's what he says:

> I will set out and go back to my father and say to him: 'Father, I have sinned against heaven and against you. I am no longer worthy to be called your son; make me like one of your hired servants.' (Luke 15:18–19)

Notice he is right in what he says – he has indeed sinned and he is indeed not worthy to be called his father's son. Those things are true. This is the admission we spent the last chapter looking at, and we have to be prepared to make exactly the same admission ourselves. We have sinned, and we are not worthy.

But back to the amazing father! When his son appears over the horizon, what does the father do? Start preparing his 'I told you so' speech? Start the biggest ticking off lecture of a lifetime? Start the long list of conditions of staying at home and paying back the money? Not a bit of it! We read this:

> While he was still a long way off, his father saw him and was filled with compassion for him; he ran to his son, threw his arms around him and kissed him. The son said to him, 'Father, I have sinned against heaven and against you. I am no longer worthy to be called your son.' But the father said to his servants, 'Quick! Bring the best robe and put it on him. Put a ring on his finger and sandals on his feet. Bring the fattened calf and kill it. Let's have a

feast and celebrate. For this son of mine was dead and is alive again; he was lost and is found.' So they began to celebrate. (Luke 15:20–24)

First, the father is filled with compassion for his lost son – he feels for him. Second, he runs to him – which was very undignified in those days and shows his great desire to welcome him home. Third, he hugs him and kisses him showing his love and welcome. Fourth, he doesn't even let him finish his speech and offer to become a servant, but interrupts to call his servants. Fifth, he immediately restores him to the position of son – signified by the robe and the ring. And sixth, he calls a great feast to celebrate his son's return.

Jesus wants his listeners to understand that the amazing father in the story is God, and the response he has to his son is the way God responds to us when we return to him. It is a picture of God's wonderful compassion to us and his ridiculous willingness to welcome and restore us.

And here too is an incredible picture of who we are as those who've come back to God – we should be only too aware of our shameful past, and yet also wonderfully aware of the privilege and blessing poured out on us. Our humble dignity as children of God is restored. We could stop there, because in that one story we see the big picture of who we are as those saved by God. But we need to unpack this further and absorb it more deeply.

The past is gone

When we become Christians, God wipes away our sin. The wonder of the gospel is that God places all of it on Jesus and punishes him in our place. Jesus is made sin for us (2 Corinthians 5:21). We're freed from our position of condemnation and instead we're forgiven and washed clean. And so everything changes – no longer do we labour under shame because our guilty past is gone.

We can shout with David, 'Blessed are those whose transgressions are forgiven, whose sins are covered' (Psalm 32:1).

We can shout with Paul, 'If anyone is in Christ, the new creation has come: The old has gone, the new is here!' (2 Corinthians 5:17).

We can shout with John, 'If we confess our sins, he is faithful and just and will forgive our sins and purify us from all unrighteousness' (1 John 1:9).

This means the true guilt we have before God is removed from us. It's gone for good because God has done away with it on the cross! It is buried with Jesus and we've been raised with him to a new guilt-free life.

Our family has a favourite memory verse (at least I do and it's forced on my children). It is Psalm 103, verse 12 which says, 'As far as the east is from the west, so far has he removed our transgressions from us.' When we look at that verse together I usually ask my children a question, 'How far away has he taken our sins?' And they reply, 'As far as the east is from the west!' 'And how far is that?' I ask. And we stretch out our arms in opposite directions and we say, 'From over there, to over there; it's a really, really long way.' The point I'm trying to make to them is that our sins really are gone!

Here's God's solution for our sin and our shame: we admit our uncleanness and then we have it wiped away, rather than pretending it doesn't exist. We must not reassure ourselves that we're 'not that bad really'. Rather, we admit that we really are bad and then see Jesus taking responsibility for our crimes.

So the writer to the Hebrews says:

> . . . let us draw near to God with a sincere heart in full assurance
> of faith, having our hearts sprinkled to cleanse us from a guilty

conscience and having our bodies washed with pure water. (Hebrews 10:22)

We can draw close to God knowing our past is washed away. We don't have to play 'let's pretend' with him, but rather we can come to him in sincerity and assurance; we can stand before him with a clear conscience.

Do you remember from the last chapter the two Bible characters who had low views of themselves? Isaiah was one – when he saw God he cried out, 'Woe is me!' But the next thing that happens is that a seraph (a sort of angel) touches his lips with a coal from the altar in the temple. And the seraph says, 'See this has touched your lips; your guilt is taken away and your sin atoned for' (Isaiah 6:7). Isaiah is being told, you are sinful and you should cry out in woe, but now your sin has been removed and paid for. It's gone. And so there's no need to cry out any more.

The other character we mentioned was the tax collector in one of Jesus' parables. He wouldn't even look up to heaven but beat his chest and, 'God, have mercy on me, a sinner.' But what was Jesus' conclusion about him? He said that the tax collector went home 'justified before God' (Luke 18:14). He would have said to him, 'Yes you are a sinner, but you're OK with God now; you can look up to heaven without beating your chest.'

The new has come

Not only is the old life gone, but a new life has started. Paul writes that the old has gone *and* the new has come – we are part of God's new creation in Christ (2 Corinthians 5:17). And so we not only have our old shameful identity forgiven and washed away, we also have a new identity in Christ.

Here's a list of things that are true of you if you are a Christian. Read it slowly. Why not put your name at the start and read it out loud?

- I have been justified freely (Romans 3:24)
- I am a new creation (2 Corinthians 5:17)
- I am seated with Christ in the heavenly realms (Ephesians 2:6)
- I have been washed and sanctified (1 Corinthians 6:11)
- I face no condemnation (Romans 8:1)
- I have been adopted as God's child (Galatians 4:5)
- I have received the Spirit to call God 'Father' (Romans 8:15)
- I am a joint heir with Christ (Romans 8:17)
- I have been made righteous in Christ (2 Corinthians 5:21)
- I have confidence to approach God (Hebrews 10:19)
- I have been redeemed by the precious blood of Jesus (1 Peter 1:18–19)
- I am part of God's chosen people and holy nation (1 Peter 2:9)
- I have been made a priest and a member of God's kingdom (Revelation 1:6)
- I am called a brother or sister by Jesus (Hebrews 2:11)

Do you see what is now given to us in Christ? Do you see our new identity? These truths now define us.

This is something for us to rejoice in and celebrate. We are truly dignified in Jesus. This makes a big and wonderful difference: a high self-image is usually related to confidence in yourself. Your estimation of yourself is one you are happy with and so you feel sure of yourself. But the Christian has confidence only in *who they are in Christ*. They are confident not of themselves but in what God has done for them and made true of them.

Theologian Anthony Hoekema puts it well:

> The Christian is not to think of himself apart from Christ as someone worthy of high esteem. But the image the Christian should have of himself is of someone who is in Christ and is therefore a new creature. The proper Christian self-image, in other words, does not imply pride in ourselves but rather glorying in what Christ has done for us and continues to do for us.

Humble dignity regained

Back in the parable of the amazing father, we saw that the son was reinstated as a son. His privileged position was regained. There was no probation period, no condition, and no payback. This is the incredible truth of the gospel of grace. Not only is the past gone and our guilt washed away, but we are lifted up.

We often think that the cross means we're forgiven, but we don't always realize it means we're loved. We can easily think that it is as if we've moved from being guilty into some 'neutral zone'. We were in God's bad books, and now we're out of them, but we're not in his good books. Perhaps we think that now all depends on how well we live for him. But that's not the true gospel of grace.

In the gospel we're not simply off the hook, but we're welcomed into the family. We're not simply no longer condemned, but we're treasured and valued by God. The son in the parable was *restored* to his position of honour. Here's the thing – God not only deals with Christ as we deserved and so punishes him on the cross, he also deals with us as Christ deserved and so blesses us as his children. We don't move to a neutral zone, but instead we're embraced by God and showered with his blessing.

The Christian should not only feel grateful for forgiveness from sin, but should also revel in the position of dignity and honour that God has given. God said to his people in the Old Testament that he rescued them from slavery and so enabled them to 'walk with heads held high' (Leviticus 26:13). Isn't that a great phrase! God saves us for the honour of being his people and so being able to hold our heads high.

It is not that we say we were worth saving at all or that we had anything to do with it, but we do say that we were saved *for magnificence*. It's like someone taking scrap metal that was only going to be thrown away and melted down, and rather than simply saving it from destruction they then transform it into something beautiful. That is God's work on us – we are saved from condemnation, but saved for the dignity and beauty of being his children.

A friend of mine has a good way of getting this across. He asks people one question to see if they really understand this: 'How does God feel about you today?' How would you answer that? How does God feel about *you*?

His answer is, 'Delighted!' If we are Christians, and so are in Christ, then God feels *delighted* with us. The reason is that he sees us as he sees Christ. He sees us as perfectly obedient, adopted children, blameless before him.

God taking delight in us

As an example, just consider the little-read book of Zephaniah:

> The LORD your God is with you,
>   the Mighty Warrior who saves.
> He will take great delight in you;
>   in his love he will no longer rebuke you,
>   but will rejoice over you with singing. (Zephaniah 3:17)

It's important to know that earlier in this chapter the sin of God's people was being exposed – they were described as those who were eager to act corruptly in all they did (Zephaniah 3:7). These were not nice guys! But in the verse above God is describing what he will do when he acts in salvation for them. Do you see what he says? He says he'll delight in them, he'll no longer rebuke them, and he'll rejoice over them. It's the same picture of the amazing Father in the parable rejoicing over his son.

The sixteenth-century reformer Martin Luther wrote about how God delighted in those who trusted in Jesus:

> If faith in Christ is present, he is delighted at my beauty which he himself has conferred on me. Therefore I ought not to doubt that I am altogether lovely for the sake of Christ.

Not that it's got anything to do with our being intrinsically delightful or lovely, but it rests on what we are in Christ. Do you see the wonderful privilege and dignity that is ours? We're restored as God's chosen people, his treasured possession that he delights in.

I can't believe it

It may be, however, that you struggle to take this on board. It sounds great, you might say, but I can't believe – it really is too good actually to be true. One of the most common reasons for this is our awareness of our sin. Some of us have trouble in believing God would really be this good to us, that our sins really are forgiven, let alone that we're restored to a position of honour.

We can particularly struggle with this because of what we think are 'big' sins, where we've done something really bad, or 'frequent' sins, where we do something very often. You may remember the student I mentioned in the last chapter who said that his mind was like a sewer. He really found it hard to believe that God delighted in him.

Here's where we need to remind ourselves about God. God knew all about us before he sent Jesus to die for us. He knew all about what we'd done and what we would do. He knows the depth of your sin far better than you do: all the sins you aren't even aware of, all the sins you have yet to think of committing. And it was with that perfect knowledge that he sent Jesus to die for you. Not just for other people, but for you.

The old church father Augustine said it well: 'God loves you as though you are the only person in the world, and he loves everyone the way he loves you.' And he loved you like that, knowing all about you. And so there can never be a time when God says, 'That sin is too bad,' or, 'That sin has been committed once too often.'

Think of two events involving Jesus and Peter. Jesus knew Peter would commit a 'bad' sin – he would deny that he even knew Jesus. And he would do it three times. But Jesus promised restoration to Peter before it had even happened (see Mark 14:27–30). He does the same with us.

Think of when Peter asked Jesus how many times he should forgive someone. He suggested it might be up to seven times – thinking he was being really generous. But Jesus said, 'Not seven times but seventy-seven times' (Matthew 18:22). Of course Jesus didn't mean seventy-eight was one too many. His point was that you don't put a number on it, you just keep on forgiving. And you do so because that is how God forgives us. There is no maximum number after which there is no more forgiveness to come.

The bottom line for us in this is believing the truth of the gospel. The danger we face is mixing the truth of the gospel with my own efforts: I think Jesus had to die for me *and* I need to add a little bit of my own work for God. That is both wrong and fatal for how I view myself.

It's wrong because God has done everything necessary for my forgiveness in Christ. It is fatal for how I view myself because now I'm committed to seeing myself as offering God something. I feel I must find something good and worthy about myself. If I do, then I can start to feel OK and hold my head up high. But if I don't, then I feel terrible about myself and hang my head in shame.

Then I start to say that God won't forgive, 'because I'm not good enough' or 'because I don't deserve it'. But those phrases give us away – of course we're not good enough, of course we don't deserve it, and that's why we need forgiveness. But we so easily slide into thinking we need to deserve it, at least a little bit, and then feel worried when we think we might not be good enough.

I must relate to God only through the cross and resurrection of Jesus. I must look at Jesus and know that I died with him and my sins were paid for. I must look at Jesus and know that I have been raised with him and have new life with God where I am accepted and dignified as his adopted child. I must resist the accusations of Satan, who will whisper lies in my ears about being 'too bad', or sinning 'too often'.

Is this really real?

As well as struggling to accept our dignity in Christ because of our sin, we can also struggle because it can feel like a huge game of 'let's pretend'. God says, 'Let's pretend you are really righteous and clean from sin; let's pretend that you are justified and are adopted.' But we feel that in reality we are far from it!

And we need to say to ourselves and to each other that this *is* true of us as we are in Christ. Understood properly, this is no game. When God declares these things he isn't pulling the wool over our eyes – it's simply that this is who we are in Christ, not in ourselves.

One of the problems we have is that these truths can be remote to us. We read or hear these words but they don't sink into us as realities. In teaching on this topic I know that people have said they believe these truths but it doesn't make any difference. Lucy expressed it well: 'It's hard to believe these things sometimes, particularly when life seems so hard. I know they are true but they are hard to hang on to.'

I also know some people end up feeling guilty for not believing this more! Sharon said explicitly: 'I feel guilty that I know God feels this way, yet although I understand and know this, I still don't feel loved by God and don't experience his love.'

If you can identify with that statement, please don't beat yourself up over it. God doesn't want you to feel guilty over it – but he does want you to be able to embrace and rejoice in these truths. The best thing I can suggest is to try to dwell deliberately on them. Take a few of the verses mentioned above and memorize them. Take a moment each day to remind yourself of them.

Say to yourself, 'As far as the east is from the west, so far has my sin been removed from me.'

Say to yourself, 'God takes great delight in me and rejoices over me with singing.'

Say to yourself, 'I am restored as a child of God – Jesus is not ashamed to call me his brother / sister.'

Picture yourself as that prodigal son coming home. Consider the welcome of the father. See him running to you; feel his embrace around you and his kisses on your head. Think about the ring being slid onto your finger and the robe being placed on your shoulders. Hear the father calling for a feast and saying that he is celebrating over you!

This is one of those areas where, once we have the truth

clear in our minds, we need to let it sink into our hearts. Pray over these things. Sing about them in praise to God. Discuss the wonder of them with your friends. Ask God by his Spirit to convince and convict you of the truth of them.

Here are some reflections from individuals as they considered this – I hope they will help you.

- 'Incomprehensible. We often have conditions to forgiveness and we still remember the wrongs someone has done to us. God is not like that – that is amazing.'
- 'I feel joyful and loved and full of praise to Christ.'
- 'The holy, righteous, perfect Son of God is not ashamed of me as a brother. I can be ashamed of me but he is not. This is amazing.'
- 'This frees me to be who I really am and not who I think I ought to be based on the world's standards. It completely amazes me, the lavish generosity and grace poured out on me, so undeserved.'
- 'I can't believe it; it's too good to be true.'
- 'I feel baffled in many ways; I utterly rejected him, yet he rejoices and welcomes me back as a prince.'
- 'What a relief, I'm restored. What a privilege.'

Questions for reflection or discussion

1. What strikes you about how God responds when we return to him?
2. Do you see yourself as being saved *for* a position of honour as well as *from* a position of condemnation?
3. How do you feel about the idea of God delighting in you?
4. What difference does it make to know that our honour and dignity are only ours in Jesus?
5. Do you struggle to believe these things? If so, why, and how can you respond?

6. accepting acceptance

Orientation is everything

Occasionally I put together bits of flat-packed furniture. I sit on the floor surrounded by pieces of wood, screws and tools. I'm usually holding a diagram in one hand and a curiously shaped piece of metal in the other. And I'm usually turning the piece of metal around in the air while mumbling to myself, 'Does it go this way or that way?'

When putting furniture together, I've learnt from painful experience that orientation is everything. The right piece can be in the right place but it must also be fitted the right way round. Otherwise it just doesn't work like it's supposed to. The same is true of the wonderful dignity we have in Christ – we have to get that truth in the right orientation.

We've seen the new identity that we have in Christ. He takes our shame and guilt and gives us his righteousness; we are crowned with glory and honour. We have been dignified. But we must make this truth speak of how great and loving

God is, rather than of how deserving and worthy we are. We must make it orientate around God rather than around us.

This might sound pretty obvious but I'm afraid it's not. Many people take these truths and orientate them in a way that centres on us. It may be done unwittingly, but it is done nevertheless. Consider the following quote:

> Many Christians' self-esteem is terribly low. They somehow
> have not come to the place of seeing how precious they are to
> God. They even wonder how God could love such a person as
> themselves. They're amazed that God forgave their sins in the
> first place.

I wonder if this writer realizes what he's written. I hope we've seen that we are indeed precious to God, but not because we're so valuable and lovely! The truth is that we *should* wonder that God could love such a person as us! We *should* be amazed that he forgave us our sins.

If we lose that sense of wonder and amazement, then we're saying that it is only right that God loves us and forgives us. Compare the opening line of the classic hymn:

> Amazing grace! How sweet the sound
> That saved a wretch like me!

That encapsulates the sense of wonder we should have.

Here is where we must draw the distinction between being 'loved' and being 'lovable'. Unfortunately our culture equates these two. If you are loved, we're told, it must be because you are lovable in some way. You are loved because of something about *you*! Not with God. We are greatly loved by God, but only because he is so loving, not because we are so lovable.

This is why we must speak of our sin and his love at the same time. I've already mentioned the tendency to play down our sin. You can see it in some revisions to old hymns like the one just quoted above. There's a new version around where the second line says, 'That saved a *soul* like me.' Why the change? Because we're told we shouldn't think of ourselves as 'wretches', since that's too demeaning.

But John Newton, who wrote the hymn, was a slave trader who knew that he was a wretch who deserved nothing from God. It was because he understood this so well that he grasped how amazing God's grace was. We must hold together our sinfulness and God's goodness because then we will see the wonder of the gospel; it will make us think big thoughts of God, not of us. Then we'll get the orientation right.

What does Jesus' death tell us?

Sometimes people speak about the cross and what it means we are worth. They say something like: 'Christ died for us, and he wouldn't have done that unless we were really worth something.' Here's one person reflecting on what they are worth because of the cross:

> I have the assurance that I am worth a lot. Christ died on the cross for me. If he thinks that much of me, I had better start thinking something good about myself.

This reveals a similar problem to the one above. There is something right about it, but the problem is its orientation. God did indeed send Jesus to die for me. But did he do so because we are worth a lot? Does the cross tell us how valuable we are?

No – not at all! There are two mistakes here. First, some say that it's a simple matter of the price telling us what something is worth. God 'paid' the death of Jesus for us and so that is our value. That argument is wrong because our position isn't one of being bought from a shop, but of being criminals whose punishment needs to be paid. If someone breaks the law, a really large fine doesn't tell them how valuable they are! It only tells them how bad the crime was. So one writer says:

> The astronomical price of our redemption is a testimony not to how good we are, but to how bad we really are. If we hadn't been so bad, a lower price would have been sufficient.

Secondly, if we follow the line of thinking above (that the cross tells me I am worth a lot), we end up saying that we really were *worth* the death of Jesus and God simply got what he paid for at the cross. If that is true, I should say to myself, 'I was worth the death of God's only Son.' No, I shouldn't dare say such a thing.

Now I want to say very quickly that God did decide the death of his Son was a price he was prepared to pay! And that tells us how wonderfully loved we are. The wonder of the cross is that God paid such a high price when we weren't worth it.

As we read the Bible, we find that Jesus dying for us is never used as evidence of our value but only as evidence that God is incredibly loving. Look at the following verses and see what the cross teaches us:

> But God demonstrates his own love for us in this: while we were still sinners, Christ died for us. (Romans 5:8)

> At one time we too were foolish, disobedient, deceived and enslaved by all kinds of passions and pleasures. We lived in malice and envy, being hated and hating one another. But when the

kindness and love of God our Saviour appeared, he saved us, not because of righteous things we had done, but because of his mercy. (Titus 3:3–5)

This is love: not that we loved God, but that he loved us and sent his Son as an atoning sacrifice for our sins. (1 John 4:10)

The cross teaches us how loving God is. If it teaches us anything about ourselves, it is only to remind us what we deserved because of our sin. So as one writer said, 'The cross of Christ should make us feel worse about ourselves and better about God.'

So we must let the cross tell us how completely forgiven and accepted we are; how we are restored and honoured in Jesus. But we let those things revolve around God not us. The gospel will not be twisted into saying something about our worth, much as we might want to shape it that way. Counsellor and writer David Powlison writes:

The true Gospel does not allow God's love to be sucked into the vortex of the soul's lust for acceptability and worth in and of itself.

Rather, the true gospel humbles us. It humbles us by saying there is nothing about us that made us worthy of salvation. It humbles us even further by saying that someone else has done all the work necessary for us to be accepted. It is humbling, but it is also absolutely wonderful!

Accepting acceptance
I've taken the heading for this chapter from a phrase by a theologian called Paul Tillich. I should probably say that unfortunately I wouldn't recommend much of his writing, but he does have some wonderful insights on grace. And

he has taught me this truth with his brilliant phrase, 'accepting acceptance'. He says that the challenge each of us faces is this: 'Accepting that you are accepted despite being unacceptable.'

Do you see that? We need to accept God's work of making us 'acceptable' in Christ even though we are actually unacceptable in ourselves. We need to accept his restoration even despite our unworthiness. We need to accept his lavish love of us, despite our unloveliness.

Our problem, though, is that we want to be acceptable in and of ourselves. Paul Tillich goes on: 'Why do I still find it so hard to accept acceptance? Is it the pride that is the root of all my sin?'

I know it is for me! We should realize that this is a hard step for our sinful hearts. Sin tells me that I am worthy and deserving in and of myself, but the gospel tells me I am unworthy and undeserving. Sin revolves around pride – which is thinking big thoughts about myself. But the gospel means being humbled and thinking small thoughts of myself and big thoughts of God.

If I would lay down my pride that insists that I have great worth and significance in and of myself, then God crowns me with his glory and honour. But I have to let him do it for me. Only then can I rejoice in it. I must accept his acceptance of me.

When talking with people about their self-image, it is this acceptance that has been a turning point. We usually need to get to the point where we actually admit we'd quite like the gospel to say something nice about us, realize it doesn't, and then realize how wonderful God's acceptance is. A friend called Ben said, 'I am reluctant over this because I still want to say I was worth it. But when it sinks in, I am reassured and it is amazing.'

As Alison reflected on this she summed it up well:

On the one hand it is a fantastic freedom to know that you are unconditionally loved; something you could never get anywhere else. However it is hard to come to terms with the fact that this is not because of you; our human nature fights for a need to feel worthy because of something nice about us.

Ultimate security

Sally was in a seminar on self-image I was leading. After we'd covered some of this stuff about accepting acceptance, she wrote: 'I am happy to be accepted despite being unacceptable because it means I am loved. That gives me security, as I know that I can be honest with God about my sin and it will be forgiven because he loves me.'

She has pinpointed a wonderful truth in being accepted despite being unacceptable – the security of our position in Christ. We are loved despite our failures, and so will continue to be loved. Our view of ourselves should be one of being wonderfully loved and accepted despite ourselves.

And that means there is great freedom here. Having realized that God's goodness towards me doesn't reflect back on how worthy I am, having realized that I'm accepted despite myself, I can then delight in it as truly unconditional love.

We are to revel in who we are in Christ, knowing that it is precisely because it is not about me that these things are secure. If God had done this because I was really quite lovable, what happens if he finds out I'm not? If God did this because I'm worth it, what if I fail him? This allows us to be honest about ourselves and yet confident in God. We must be willing for him to pass his verdict of 'guilty and wicked sinner' and then his verdict of 'justified and loved child'.

We so often take two truths, my sinfulness and God's loving acceptance, and make them opposites that need to balance each other. If I'm feeling a bit down on myself, I should remind myself that God loves me and accepts me. If I'm feeling a bit big for my boots, I should remember my sin. But these aren't opposites that we must balance; they are a pair that walk hand in hand and reinforce each other.

As counsellor Paul Tournier says: 'Believers who are the most desperate about themselves are the ones who express most forcefully their confidence in grace.' That's what we need: an awareness of the seriousness of our sin that makes us run to trust and rejoice in God's grace alone.

Jack said: 'It's not about me, so it's not down to me. I don't have to earn it and I don't deserve it, so it can't be taken away by my bad performance or sinful ways. That's just incredible. I am given Jesus' righteousness and he pays for my sin, so I can be accepted in spite of who I am – WOW!'

Similarly Lucy spoke of the peace we can have in knowing these truths: 'This is the only source of peace. If I had to make myself acceptable, it would be a source of despair. As it is, the pressure is off – I am accepted, because I am forgiven.'

Ultimate stability

We can walk two paths here. We can try to prove that we are acceptable on our own terms, or we can admit our guilt and accept God's acceptance of us. If we walk the first path we live a very unstable life. It's the life where how I feel all depends on what I've done, how well I've done it, how I've looked, who I've met, and on it goes.

Some days I might feel good about myself – I've looked competent, I've been admired, I've lost weight, I've been complimented, or whatever it is that works for me. Another day, or in fact minutes later the same day, I feel bad about myself – I've been criticized or I've failed, I've seen someone trendier than me, I've eaten more than I meant to, or whatever it is that gets me down.

When asked to describe his view of himself, Steve wrote a series of single words like this: insecure/arrogant, insignificant/proud, useless/great, intelligent/stupid. I can relate to that. These all come from walking this path: when I'm doing well I tend towards pride; when I'm doing badly I tend towards self-pity.

The key thing to see is that what we are after is not some middle position between those two. What we are after is a different way of thinking about ourselves. We need to walk the path of admitting our guilt and failure and accepting God's acceptance of us. Then we are stable in who we are, despite the success and failures and comparisons of the day. The difference between the two is shown in the diagram below.

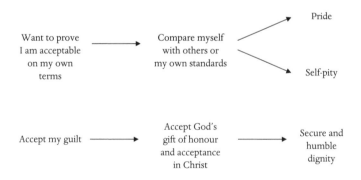

When I walk the second path and accept God's acceptance, then I am not only secure but I am also stable. I'm not thrown by the feedback of the mirrors of the world around me whether that makes me feel good or bad about myself. I know who I am, and I have constant humble dignity.

Loving the adulterer (that's you, by the way)

Imagine a wife who commits adultery. Not just a one-night stand or a foolish moment. Think of considered and deliberate unfaithfulness. Imagine, though, that rather than giving up on her, her husband tries to win her back. Imagine that he is loving and kind and draws her back into relationship with him, and one day she returns.

Now just think about the attitude she would have in returning. She can't go back to him while saying to herself that he is lucky to have her, can she? She can't go back with her head held high in defiance. She can't even go back thinking she can repay her debt to him. *She can only go back accepting his acceptance of her.* She can only return, humble and grateful he has been so kind.

She would say to her friends, 'It was all because of *him*; he saved our marriage.' She would use phrases like, 'I didn't deserve it.' Being back together would speak well of him, not of her.

Why have I got you to think about such a scenario? Because this is exactly the picture used in the Bible to describe our relationship with God. God is the husband and we, his people, are his bride. But we commit adultery. The adultery is our spiritual unfaithfulness where we turn away from God and run after other gods. That was one of God's most heart-rending cries against Israel.

But despite Israel's adultery, God will marry her again. Here's the husband who will have his unfaithful wife back. In fact he'll love her and draw her back. This is what is pictured so dramatically in the book of Hosea, where Hosea himself, the prophet, is told to go and marry a promiscuous woman – a wife who is then unfaithful to him. Why is he told to do something that would cause him such great personal pain?

It is an acted-out picture of God's relationship with his people. And so, after all her unfaithfulness to him, Hosea is told to go and love his wife again. Here's the incredible picture of God's love for us:

> The LORD said to me, 'Go, show your love to your wife again, though she is loved by another and is an adulteress. Love her as the LORD loves the Israelites, though they turn to other gods.'
> (Hosea 3:1)

Hosea and his wife act as a worked example of us and God. We have been adulterous. We are guilty of the most profound unfaithfulness. But God comes and loves us again. He still takes us to be his bride.

I've mentioned this picture of God loving the adulterer to try to drive home this idea of accepting our acceptance. When we see the situation like this, we realize that the gospel is not about how worthy we are, but about how wonderful God is. All we can do is admit our adultery, admit that there is nothing lovely or deserving about us, and accept his love and acceptance of us. This is not to undermine anything we saw in the last chapter – we must go on to rejoice in his acceptance of us, we must revel in the fact he saved us for himself and delights in us. We must simply make it orientate around him.

Accepting acceptance in practice
We've seen that the gospel calls us to accept God's acceptance of us. Let's think through some examples of what this means in practice.

You just need to accept yourself for who you are
If you do any reading on the topic of self-image or identity, you'll soon discover a truism that everyone seems to put forward: you need to accept yourself for who you are.

Christians can't agree. We know that we have no reason to accept ourselves. We know we only have reason to despise our sinfulness. Any attempt at 'self-acceptance' means deceiving myself as to what I am really like. In addition 'self-acceptance' means making myself my own judge. It means saying I decide whether or not I make the grade. But who am I to decide such things? I should be much more concerned about the opinion and judgment of the one who made me. And so the Christian will reject all encouragements to 'just accept yourself for who you are'.

But I hope you can see that there is a way in which I can accept myself. I know God loves and accepts me despite myself. So there can and should be self-acceptance – but only in Christ. I don't finally come to accept that I'm OK in myself, rather I come to accept that God has made me OK – more than OK! I accept the dignity he gives me in Christ.

I can't forgive myself

Have you ever heard someone say, 'I just can't forgive myself'? It's usually when they feel they've done something particularly bad. When someone says that it sounds like they are being very humble, maybe even spiritual. They certainly sound very down on themselves.

It may be that when someone says 'I can't forgive myself' they are simply expressing their despair over their sin and they need to realize the full and free forgiveness from God that we've been talking about. But it's usually said in a situation where the person knows about God's forgiveness and they say, 'God may forgive me, but I'll never forgive myself.' That's actually another way of saying I am not willing to accept acceptance from God.

Just think through what is happening. When I say I can't forgive myself I am making myself two things. I am making myself the dispenser of forgiveness; the one who can offer it. And I am making myself the recipient of forgiveness who can decide if it is deserved and whether it should be accepted. It's like being in debt and then saying to yourself that you could offer yourself money to pay off the debt but that you didn't think you should accept it from yourself. It's ridiculous!

Biblically I sin against someone else and they offer me forgiveness which I accept. So if I say that I refuse to forgive myself, I'm in danger of saying that my standards and conditions for forgiveness are higher than God's and I know better than him.

I know that when such thoughts go through my mind, what I'm expressing is that I really want to meet my own standards or prove myself acceptable. I don't want to accept that I've failed or admit my inability. So what I do is chew over my mistakes and dwell on my sin in self-recrimination. What I'm really saying is, 'I can't believe that I did that – I can't accept that that was me.'

Which means that when I say, 'I can't forgive myself', I'm in danger of not accepting God's acceptance of me despite myself. I want to make it on my own, not humbly admit my failure and accept God's grace.

God accepts me as I am

There's another commonly quoted phrase in the Christian world that's worth mentioning here. It's a phrase which is usually offered when someone is feeling down on themselves. A friend comfortingly says, 'Remember God accepts you just as you are.'

As with most truisms, there is something absolutely right about this. The wonderful truth is that God doesn't ask us to change before we come to him. He doesn't tell us to sort ourselves out and then he'll have us. No, he meets us where we are and lifts us up. That is absolutely and wonderfully true and we should remind ourselves – God accepts us without us changing ourselves.

But sometimes people say, 'God accepts me as I am', meaning that I'm acceptable now, just as I am. It is taken to imply that I'm good enough for God already. But that's rubbish – nothing could be further from the truth. God doesn't actually accept me as I am; he accepts me as I am *in Christ*. He calls me to admit that I'm not acceptable just as I am, but then to accept the glorious honour he gives to me.

Looking in the mirror

As I look in the mirror, I now have a choice as to how to see myself. I can focus on who I am within myself – my identity is the shameful admission of a sinner. Or I can look at myself as who I am in Christ. I can look at myself and say, 'You were washed, you were sanctified, you were justified in the name of the Lord Jesus Christ' (1 Corinthians 6:11).

The challenge for Christians is to think of themselves in terms of their new identity in Christ. We've said that this isn't an instantaneous move we can make. We can't throw off patterns of thought in a moment. But this is who we are, this is how we should see ourselves, this is the identity we must work through.

But the point of this chapter has been that one reason we find this hard is because it means not looking at ourselves but at Christ. It should be pretty clear by now that the gospel provides no back-door route to thinking well of ourselves on our own terms. Our dignity in creation was still a dignity derived from God. How much more so the dignity of our new identity in Christ! And so to realize this new identity, we must focus our eyes on Jesus.

And so I must look in the mirror and tell myself, 'I am accepted by God because of Jesus.' And I must accept that acceptance. That means time spent dwelling on God's acceptance of me and his love to me, making it revolve around him and not me.

Questions for reflection or discussion

1. When do you feel most amazed at God's love and forgiveness to you? Why?
2. When we look at the cross of Jesus, what should we think and feel about ourselves, and think and feel about God?
3. What are your reflections on being accepted despite being unacceptable? Why might you find it hard to accept this?
4. What freedom do we gain when we realize we are accepted despite ourselves?
5. Do you hear people saying you should accept yourself or forgive yourself? What is right and wrong about this?
6. How will you continue to keep the truth of the gospel in the right orientation?

7. living the new life

How should I feel today?

Debbie has had a good Saturday: she had fun with the kids in the morning doing crafts and reading at home. She'd been struggling with the kids recently and had been snapping at her youngest child, but that was kept well in check and everyone was happy. In the afternoon she went to the house of a friend who was having a mini-financial crisis – Debbie knows about such things and could give helpful and reassuring advice. The friend was very grateful for her kindness and practical help. It's been a good day. How should Debbie feel?

Dan has had a bad Saturday. He fell out with his house mates over breakfast because the discussion about whose turn it was to do the washing up went pear-shaped once again. He said some things he now feels bad about. Then he lost his temper playing football, made a rash challenge and got sent off. It's been a bad day. How should Dan feel?

As a Christian, how should I now think about what I do and achieve in life? Is it wrong for me to take pride in my work or my successes? Should I feel bad about my ongoing failures? We'll think first about our obedience or lack of obedience in living godly lives. Then we'll move to all we do, or don't do, in serving God.

Living to please God

Paul says he is praying for the Christians in Colossae. This is what he prays:

> We continually ask God to fill you with the knowledge of his will through all the wisdom and understanding that the Spirit gives, so that you may live a life worthy of the Lord and please him in every way . . . (Colossians 1:9–10)

Christians are people who can now live lives that please God and are worthy of him. That's what Paul wants to see in the Colossians' lives and so that's what he prays for.

We can please God by:

- showing love and kindness to those around us rather than thinking only of ourselves (Ephesians 4:32);
- resisting lust and being pure in our relationships (Ephesians 5:3);
- working with integrity in our employment, studies, home responsibilities (Colossians 3:22–24);
- being good and caring parents, and/or children who honour their parents (Ephesians 6:1–4);
- being content with what we have rather than being consumed with greed (1 Timothy 6:6–7);
- only speaking what is helpful to people rather than gossip and lies (Ephesians 4:25, 29);

- being generous with money and good deeds for the benefit of others (1 Timothy 6:18);
- putting up with people and forgiving them rather than giving in to anger and bitterness (Ephesians 4:2).

And the list could go on. The bottom line is that, as those who've been re-created in Jesus and adopted into God's family with his Spirit in us, we can please God by living obedient, godly, faithful lives – in every area of life. So how should we feel about pleasing God?

I obeyed God . . . well actually, God did

My wife and I have three children. They are great but prone to all the usual kid stuff. We work away in bringing them up – telling them to share, to be kind, to think of others, not to lie, not to hit, and on and on it goes. Sometimes I watch them and I see one of them doing something very kind or generous. How do I feel in that moment? I feel *pleased*! I smile and think, 'That's great.' When I get a chance later on I'll tell my wife about it.

Similarly, when we talk about living to please God, that does mean *God is pleased* – God smiles down on our obedience. It's what he wants to see from his children. As a result, there is a sense in which we should feel 'good' about living for God.

But think a bit more about it. When we obey God, we are only doing what we ought to do. He made us to love and obey him and love other people. So when we do live for him we can't pat ourselves on the back and say, 'Aren't I great!' We're only doing what is right.

A football player doesn't come off from a game and boast about not cheating, or at least, he shouldn't! He is expected to play within the rules, and not breaking them isn't supposed to be a source of pride. So it is with us: we can't boast that we kept the rules today.

But I did just say we could feel 'good' about pleasing God. Yes, but that feeling 'good' is not a proud 'Well done me' sort of feeling. To use my now well-worn phrase, there is a *humble dignity* about our obedience. There's true dignity involved because we are living a life that pleases our creator. We are living the life we were designed to live in obedience to him and in loving relationship to those around us. And there is great dignity in that, but there is also humility because I am only doing what is right.

There is also humility for another reason: I can only do it because God has re-created me by his Spirit. Before that I was trapped in sin. And I can only do it because his Spirit continues to work in me to lead me and empower me to obey God.

Paul describes this in his letter to the Galatians: 'So I say live by the Spirit and you will not gratify the desires of the sinful nature . . .' 'Since we live by the Spirit, let us keep in step with the Spirit'(Galatians 5:16, 25).

Our life is now a life empowered and led by the Spirit. Our choices are still involved but the Spirit leads us to live this pleasing life. Similarly in Philippians, Paul says that God is at work in us to bring about this new life we can live (Philippians 2:12–13). And so this new life that pleases God is ultimately from God.

And so Debbie, who had a good day, should not be proud of her obedience, as if it's all down to her. But she can and should be pleased and grateful at God's work in her. She can and should delight in the dignity of living a life worthy of God.

What about all that sin in my life?

So what about Dan, who had a bad day? Well we can't and shouldn't ignore our sin. But we will continue to sin for as long as we live. Actually, Dan was only aware of the more obvious moments of his sin. In that sense, we should remind ourselves that Debbie hasn't had a perfect day – while she has been aware of pleasing God in some ways, her day has not been 'sin-free'. Such a day does not and cannot exist until Jesus returns and re-creates us so that sin is gone forever.

The issue for Dan on his bad day is whether he should now feel worse about himself and have a lower view of himself. In one sense you can see how he should: he wants to live a life pleasing God and worthy of the gospel. Comparing ourselves with that standard and seeing how far short he falls will lead to a pretty depressing feeling.

But to think that way is to forget our new identity in Christ! My sin today does not change the truths we've been thinking about so far in this book. I am still adopted as a child of God, sanctified and justified in Christ and loved by my Father.

When I become aware of my ongoing sin and failure to please God, I should be reminded of why I needed him to save me in the first place. I must tell myself that my standing with God hasn't changed. I haven't slipped down the ladder of acceptance with him. The reason I haven't and I can't is because he himself has placed me at the top of that ladder.

When I have a bad day, I should be *humbled* because I'm reminded of my rebellious nature. And as I become aware of sin, I confess it to God. But I know my acceptance with God and my honour in Christ are no different to how they were at the start of the day! And so I should also be *reassured* – my status and dignity in Christ are not down to me and how good I am.

Don't start climbing ladders with God

There is a real danger for us to think that we are saved by God's goodness and grace, but then switch to a different system and start pleasing God and earning acceptance from him. We start thinking we're climbing a ladder of acceptance.

This was a problem for a group of Christians that Paul wrote to in Galatia. Here's something Paul said to them:

> I do not set aside the grace of God, for if righteousness
> could be gained through the law, Christ died for nothing!
> (Galatians 2:21)

In this verse, Paul is talking about the ongoing Christian life and he wants to stress that he does not 'set aside the grace of God'. He doesn't think he can become a Christian by God's grace and then put that to one side. God's grace isn't the key that gets us into the building of salvation which we can then hang on a hook once we're inside. It is the foundation to the whole building – you can never set it aside and say you don't need it any more.

Paul explains himself by adding that if we could really be righteous before God by our obedience, Jesus wouldn't have had to die for us: 'if righteousness could be gained through the law, Christ died for nothing'. If we start thinking we are earning acceptance from God we're denying the cross.

There are two opposite ways of relating to God. One thinks the relationship is all about what God has done for us and given to us; what we have to do is trust and receive from him. The other thinks it is all about what we do for God and give him; what we have to do is give and trust that it's enough. Living the Christian life is carrying on with the first of these. That is the life of faith in Jesus, staying in the grace of God.

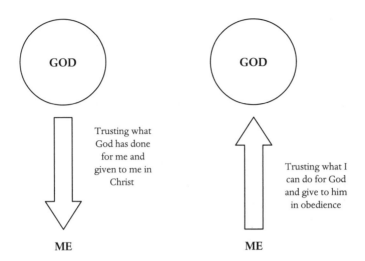

While talking to Becky about the idea of staying in grace, she said: 'Ever since I became a Christian I feel as if I have been moving away from grace; I've been led to believe that the more things you do, the more you serve, the more holy you are, the more secure you are. Then you get to a point where you can't keep that up any more and you find you have moved so far from God's grace.'

We need to beware setting aside the grace of God and starting to climb ladders of acceptance with him. We continue to live accepted by grace, despite being unacceptable.

Reflecting on a bad day

So how should Dan think about his sin on his bad day? As we've said, he should be humbled and should confess it to God and receive his forgiveness. But he must also be reassured that he is secure. He must not be tempted to start relating to God through his efforts. He should remind himself of God's grace and rely on it once again.

This is not to say we aren't bothered about our sin – there should be an ongoing fight with sin in the power of the Spirit.

Nor is it to say that God isn't bothered about our sin – he's working to remove it from our lives. But it is to say that our status is secure.

The picture of family life is helpful here. A child can live to please or displease his parents. He can obey or disobey. When he disobeys, he should come and say sorry. But his place in the family is never in question! He is and remains a dearly loved child. That is the security of our position with God.

Every time I've spoken to people about this, it has struck a chord. We all instinctively think we slide down the ladder with God. Especially when we repeat one sin over and over again. *But do not set aside the grace of God.*

So Vicky said, 'I previously felt that "more" sin in my life distanced me from God and lowered my self-image.' I think she speaks for us all. But she went on to say, 'I must remember that God's grace and mercy are constant.' That's right. We must keep our fight against sin going strong, but we must also stay in the grace of God.

Such a gifted child

Simon is a great preacher – articulate, thoughtful, passionate. Everyone at his church loves to hear him speak and they say so regularly to one another and to Simon. How should Simon feel about himself and what he does?

Sally serves coffee at her church and does so very well and pleasantly, but it's actually hard to be really great at serving coffee. People thank her as she hands the cup over but no one says how much they look forward to the week when she's on the coffee rota. How should Sally feel about herself and what she does?

These are caricatured examples but you see the issue. We've thought about how we should view our obedience or lack of obedience to God; but what about our serving him? How should we feel about what God does through us?

This is how Peter expresses it in his first letter:

Each of you should use whatever gift you have received to serve others, as faithful stewards of God's grace in its various forms. If you speak, you should do so as one who speaks the very words of God. If you serve, you should do so with the strength God provides, so that in all things God may be praised through Jesus Christ. To him be the glory and the power for ever and ever. Amen. (1 Peter 4:10–11)

Peter says we've each been gifted by God – we've each got particular abilities or skills we can use. Notice how they are to be used. He says we've received them to *serve* other people. Most people's skills and abilities in the world are used for their own advancement or so that everyone can look at them and say how great they are. But we haven't been given gifts for our own fulfilment or to receive applause for them. We've been given them for the good of other people, to serve them. Our gifts are for them, not for us.

But look at how Peter describes what is happening when we use our gifts: he says we are like 'faithful stewards' of God's grace. When he says 'stewards', he means like a manager – someone who is put in charge. If someone lent you their car or their house and you were in charge of using it well on their behalf, you would be the 'steward' of it.

And so here Peter is saying that we have been given some of God's grace, his goodness and kindness and generosity, and we are in charge of using it well in passing it on to other people. That is what is happening when we use our gifts to serve one another. We are dispensers of God's grace to other people, by faithfully using the gift he's given us.

Passing on grace

Church life then should be like a giant game of pass the parcel. We are given God's grace – his goodness and kindness – and we pass it on to other people. It is given to us for them – and a faithful steward of it passes it on.

This completely changes the way we view serving one another in the church. Imagine someone says something to you that is helpful, encouraging, clarifying, or even rebuking when needed. Or imagine someone serves you in practical care, time spent visiting, meals offered, lifts given, whatever it is.

At that moment we should think to ourselves, 'God is being gracious to me, through that person.' God is being kind, God is showing his goodness – I am receiving God's grace. I am doing so through that person speaking or that person serving, but they are a steward of God's grace – and so I look through them and see God being kind to me.

And so how should we feel in speaking to or serving one another? How should Simon feel? How should Sally feel? They should see themselves as having the wonderful privilege of passing on God's grace! And as with our obedience above, there is a sense in which we can and should feel 'pleased' about this. Our service of God is genuinely pleasing to him. Paul says that the practical service the Philippians gave him is 'a fragrant offering, an acceptable sacrifice, pleasing to God' (Philippians 4:18). There is immense dignity to this. But (you saw it coming) it is humble dignity.

This dignity remains humble because the gifts we have were given by God in the first place – they aren't actually *ours* at all. And they are given so that God can pass his grace on through us. We see ourselves as channels of grace, not the source of grace.

This understanding of gifts also means we welcome and value everyone's contribution. We all have a role to play; we all have a gift to use. People's gifts are different but they are all to serve others and they all pass on God's grace. And so there is to be no elevating of one kind of gift above another.

So Simon must be careful to remind himself of these things. He should be grateful for the chance to be a faithful steward, but not allow people's appreciation of his teaching to blind him to the fact that it is a gift from God. He must also remember that everyone else in the church is gifted too; he must appreciate Sally's gifts.

Sally should remind herself of these things too. If she feels what she is doing is a little mundane, she should remember that this is God being gracious to people through her. And she must appreciate Simon's gift as well.

I worked hard . . . well actually, God did

We can broaden this from our specific gifts to think about serving God in all we do. Here's a great statement from the apostle Paul about his service for God.

> For I am the least of the apostles and do not even deserve to be called an apostle, because I persecuted the church of God. But by the grace of God I am what I am, and his grace to me was not without effect. No, I worked harder than all of them – yet not I, but the grace of God that was with me. (1 Corinthians 15:9–10)

Paul comments on his status as an apostle – he recognizes he in no way deserves such a position, but says it is by the grace of God that he is what he is. But then he says how hard he has worked as an apostle, and in so doing compares himself with the other apostles. He says he has worked harder than all of them! It might seem to us to be a bit cheeky – saying he's done more than anyone else.

But he immediately clarifies – it wasn't him working really hard, it was God's grace with him. This is what he means by saying that God's grace to him was not without effect – that is, it resulted in his working hard in ministry. So who was working hard here? Paul or God? Well, Paul was, but only because of God's grace.

So could Paul be 'proud' of what God did through him? Can we? Elsewhere Paul comments on his work and uses a word rather like 'pride'. Here's one example about his work in the church in Thessalonica:

> For what is our hope, our joy, or the crown in which we will glory in the presence of our Lord Jesus when he comes? Is it not you? Indeed, you are our glory and joy. (1 Thessalonians 2:19–20)

Paul says he will 'glory' in these people – that is in what has been achieved in them. They are his crown! He's not embarrassed about what he's achieved, is he? But Paul has previously thanked God for how these people became Christians and have grown as Christians (see 1 Thessalonians 1:2–3; 2:13). Why? Because God is the one at work in them through Paul.

So how should Paul feel about all he has achieved? Could I suggest 'humble dignity'? Paul can have a great feeling of dignity, even pride, at what he has done, but it is humble because it was only because of God working through him.

Good and faithful servants

Jesus says we should look forward to the day when he will say to us, 'Well done, good and faithful servant' (Matthew 25:21,

23). Jesus will speak words of commendation to us about how we have lived for him – what a great moment that will be! There is real dignity in living for Jesus now and he will say, 'Well done!'

However those lines come from a parable where the master of his house gives gifts to his servants to be used well in his absence. So while they are commended for being good and faithful, they can't be proud of what they've done – because their master was the one who enabled them to do it in the first place.

This quote gets the perspective right:

> Our achievements are rightly seen as being due to God. Nevertheless they are something that God chooses to achieve through us . . . We need to value our own achievements – not to boast in them, but to value them as something God regarded as worth achieving in and through us.

We need to work hard to get this perspective in practice, though. We are brought up with the idea that we should be proud of what we achieve and use our gifts to advance ourselves. The Christian cannot think that way – whether in the church or the home or the workplace. All we can do is because of God. We can be pleased and even proud of what he does through us, but remain humble.

Here are some honest comments from people about the idea of God working through them and gifting them, and some of the challenges involved in that. Think through what your reflections are as you read them.

- 'I love the feeling when I know God has used me in someone's life; it's an absolute joy and privilege.'
- 'God is administering his grace though ordinary people

like me. Motives become all important. Do I use my car
to give that lift to someone resentfully or gladly?'

- 'I am amazed that God uses me at all. Sometimes I
  don't feel very gifted and am jealous of the way
  God has gifted others, especially if their ministry
  is public.'
- 'I feel privileged. I need to be consistent in attributing
  it to God but truthfully acknowledge my involvement
  in it.'
- 'I've become really aware of the need to use our gifts
  for God's glory. I'd like to change the way I act on this
  and become a glad participator in the gifts God's given
  me. I want to use them with joy and attribute them to
  him without becoming proud.'

Looking in the mirror

So as we look in the mirror of God's word, we find that we
have been re-created by his Spirit so we can live a life that is
pleasing to him. We find that we have been gifted so that we
can serve those around us. In both those things there is
tremendous dignity – we can live as God's children with
whom he is pleased; we can pass on his grace to others.

And so we should rightly delight in living this new life – but
not be proud about it. It is all because of him. Living for God
should mean humble dignity.

Questions for reflection or discussion

1. How do most Christians tend to feel when they are
   aware of obeying or disobeying God?
2. What change in attitude do you want to have about
   your obedience or disobedience in living for God?
3. How can you make sure you do not 'set aside the grace
   of God'?

4. How do most Christians usually regard different gifts and service for God?

5. What change in attitude do you want to have about your gifts and service?

8. the re-orientated life

You may have heard the phrase 'a Copernican revolution'. It comes from a guy called Copernicus (surprise, surprise) who discovered that the earth revolved around the sun. Up until then people thought that the earth was the centre of our solar system and everything revolved around it. Discovering that we actually rotated around something else was a massive shift in thinking that people struggled with. Some resisted it and just couldn't take it on board. The phrase 'Copernican revolution' is now used of any similar massive change in thinking where your whole understanding of something gets turned around.

Becoming a Christian involves a Copernican revolution. We come to realize that we now live for Jesus, rather than for ourselves. We discover he is the centre of life, not us. It takes time to work that one through, though. We're not used to the idea and we often resist it. We keep on putting ourselves back at the centre of our world and so have to fight to place ourselves where we belong out in orbit around Jesus.

The Christ-centred life

The apostle Paul wrote about the change of thinking that we should have because of Jesus' death. This is what he said:

> And he died for all, that those who live should no longer live for
> themselves but for him who died for them and was raised again.
> (2 Corinthian 5:15)

Jesus died so that we might no longer live for ourselves but live for him. Rather than living a life centred on me and my needs and my wants and my desires, I am now to live life centred on Jesus. My life is to be re-orientated around Jesus.

'What has this got to do with our identity?' you might be asking. Simply this: I so easily think of myself as the most important person in my life! And that means I look to other people, and even God himself, for what they will think of me and how much they will make of me. I am at the centre of my world and my desire for a 'great' identity is simply one expression of that.

Once we become Christians, of course we know there's something wrong with this. But the revolution often doesn't go deep enough. I still want glory for myself; not too much, of course, because that would be rude, and Jesus really ought to have some, but I'd like just enough to feel good about myself.

A friend and I have sometimes laughed at ourselves over this by changing the words to a well-known worship song and singing, 'It's all about me . . . and all this is for my glory and my fame.' We laugh as we do it, but we know that actually it's serious. I would quite like it to be all about me. But it can't be. It's all about Jesus (the song does actually get it right).

Jesus died so that I might no longer live for myself but for him. So I must set apart my desire to be first and I say, 'I live for

Jesus – he is the most important person in my life and I want a spotlight to shine on him, and I want him to be glorified.' And as I do so, I take my proper place in orbit around Jesus.

This is after all only how God created us in the first place. We looked earlier at how God made us to relate to him as our Creator, King and Father. The heart of sin is trying to over-turn that created pattern in putting ourselves first. So now in Jesus we return to the original design. This is fundamental to our true identity.

To put this same point differently, I can't keep on thinking about myself and my needs and then think Jesus meets them. You may remember the areas of identity or self-image we spoke about in an earlier chapter: performance of roles, pedi-gree, acceptance by others, and eternal significance. Some Christian writers simply take that list and see how they are met in Jesus. And so they tell us that we are loved and accepted by Jesus, made part of his family, gifted by him, and promised eternal life, and so on.

As I hope you've seen, there is great and wonderful truth in that, *but* we can't simply walk that route. Beginning with me and my needs and then asking Jesus to fill them keeps me at the centre. It makes Jesus revolve around me and what I want. It allows me to simply add Jesus to the list of things that might make me feel better about myself.

Instead I have to allow Jesus to redefine me totally and tell me what my needs really are. I need to bow before him, accept his work of salvation for me, put him at the centre and take my place in orbit around him.

C. S. Lewis wrote about people who might be tempted to come to Jesus for what he would give them. He said:

There must be a real giving up of the self. You must throw it away 'blindly' so to speak. Christ will indeed give you a real personality, but you must not go to him for the sake of that. As long as your personality is what you are bothering about, you are not going to him at all. The very first step is to try to forget about the self altogether.

That's right. I don't go to Jesus to get what I want – whether it's a real personality, or a feeling of being loved and valued, or a sense of belonging. I go to him as the one who saved me, and now I re-orientate myself around him.

Glorifying Jesus
This has a massive impact on how I live life. Life is no longer about glorifying me.

Just think about how we go about our work or our studies. What is my motivation? When I studied at university, it was partly because university life was fun and I had to do some study to stay there! But it was also about getting a degree so I could get a decent job, or at least a better job than otherwise. It was also so I could say to myself and to others, 'I've got a degree.' It was also to meet the expectations of my parents and please them. *So it was in fact all about me.*

What about when I started work? I worked reasonably hard for a variety of reasons. I enjoyed what I did and got some satisfaction and reward from it. I was fairly good at it and was advancing up the career ladder and feeling good about that. I liked the idea of being a success. *So it was in fact all about me.*

We could run the same ideas through relationships, hobbies, sport, socializing and so on. I lived for myself.

Now I don't mean to say that everything I did was con-sciously selfish. It's not that I didn't think of others, and didn't think of God at all. I did. It's just that the bottom line was that life revolved around me. In terms of self-image, I did loads of stuff for the sake of appearances, so as to feel better about myself. Much of life was in fact about glorifying Graham.

Do you see how profound this idea of living for Jesus is? Putting Jesus at the centre? Here's a stunning verse from Paul:

> So whether you eat or drink or whatever you do, do it all for the glory of God. (1 Corinthians 10:31)

Paul has been talking in this passage about what sort of food people were eating and why, but his point in this verse is more general. It covers 'whatever you do', eating and drinking and everything else. All of life is to be lived for the glory of God, to magnify him and not us.

This doesn't rule out enjoying the pleasures of life. It doesn't mean not working hard and doing well. It doesn't mean we can't hang out with friends, do hobbies or play sport. No, we should do and should enjoy all those things. What it does mean is not living life to bolster my self-created identity, not living life glorifying me, but rather re-orientating my life around Jesus.

We need to be honest with ourselves here and ask some hard questions. Try these:

- Why do I work in the way that I do? What am I trying to gain for myself?
- Why do I relate to my partner, friends, colleagues the way I do? What am I looking for from them?
- Why do I do the hobbies/sports/social activities I do? What do I hope to attain by them?

Please don't think I want you to go into some morbid introspective slump! And again please don't think I'm against enjoying life – God gives us good gifts to enjoy, gifts of work, friends, sport, food and everything else. What I'm after here is the examination of our hearts to see how we put ourselves at the centre. Try to spot those areas, and then confess them to God and turn from them. Take your place in orbit around Jesus – it is where we belong. It is where we will know who we really are.

The other-centred life

Being Jesus centred also means being other-person centred. We said in an earlier chapter that we were made to live under God as our king, but also in relationship with others. We live in loving community, reflecting the loving community of the Trinity – Father, Son and Spirit. This is why the most important commandment is to love God, but the second is to love our neighbour (Mark 12:29–31).

Paul writes in Philippians 2:3–5:

> Do nothing out of selfish ambition or vain conceit. Rather, in humility value others above yourselves, not looking to your own interests but each of you to the interests of the others. In your relationships with one another, have the same attitude of mind Christ Jesus had . . .

Paul goes on in this passage to talk about how Jesus, although he was God himself, made himself nothing and served us. In other words, how Jesus humbly looked to our interests rather than his own, and valued us above himself. So Paul is saying that our attitude to one another must now echo the example of Jesus. I should now live valuing other people above myself and considering how I can serve them.

This again is fundamental to our identity. We discover and live out who we really are when we love God and other people, rather than trying to focus on ourselves.

Need people less, love people more

We commented in an earlier chapter that when our identity is derived from other people it affects how we relate to them. In fact it warps and distorts relationships. What I am trying to describe is a return to how God designed us to live. And when we derive our identity from how he has made us and saved us, we are free to relate to people as we are meant to.

Just think about the differences this makes. I've tried to summarize them in the table below.

Identity from relationships and opinions	Humble dignity in Christ
Need people to affirm me	Can serve people without their affirmation
Avoid those who make me feel worse about myself	Can be with, and embrace, anyone
Respond badly to criticism	Can accept and listen to criticism
Look up to some people wishing I could be more like them	Am able to be myself
Feel threatened by those I think are better than me	Can rejoice in other people's abilities and gifts
Treat people like an audience I have to impress	Treat people as individuals I can love

The difference between the two columns is incredible. When we are restored to the humble dignity we have in Christ and live by staying in grace, we can 'need people less and love people more' (this is a great phrase from counsellor and writer Ed Welch).

Knowing who I am in Christ – unlovely but wonderfully loved and accepted – means I can relate to others as I was meant to do. I can be humble, knowing that I have no reason for pride, and yet I can be secure, because I am completely accepted in Christ. From that position I can live serving others.

Paul makes this connection in how we are to live as God's people in Colossians 3:12–14:

> Therefore, as God's chosen people, holy and dearly loved, clothe yourselves with compassion, kindness, humility, gentleness and patience. Bear with each other and forgive one another if any of you has a grievance against someone. Forgive as the Lord forgave you. And over all these virtues put on love, which binds them all together in perfect unity.

See who we are? We are God's chosen people, who are holy and dearly loved by him! As those people we now live in relationship with other people as he meant us to. My growing awareness of God's love, grace and acceptance melts away my desire for affirmation from others so I can serve them.

I'm not saying that it's easy. Rather, it's something we will work at for the rest of our lives, but it is true nonetheless. And so we need to reflect on our relationships and how we live in them. We need to be honest with ourselves and ask for God's help.

Why not ask yourself the following questions:

- Do I hope for compliments from people? Why? What do I think they will give me?
- Do I hope people will notice how well I do something? Why? What do I think that will change?
- Do I think looking good will make an impression on people? Why? How will it make a difference to my life?
- Do I long for opportunities to impress people in what I can say or do or be? Why? How will life be different if I do?

You may find yourself struggling with these questions – this can be the moment when you realize what you're doing and feel crushed. Please be reassured, God wants you to see how his grace can change this. For each of these questions above, ask yourself: how does knowing God's acceptance change this? How does knowing my humble dignity in Christ make a difference here? How can I look to love rather than need people?

Life together as God's people

We must also consider some of the crucial implications of this for the culture of Christian community – life together as church.

We've explored how we can easily live with a wrong view of our identity when we look for affirmation from others, seek to compare ourselves with others, and gain value from our status and roles. We need to be honest and say that this happens in the church as much as anywhere else. We've already mentioned in the last chapter the example of gifting, where we can worry over which gift we have compared to that of other people, or how our gift is perceived in church, whereas we want a culture that rightly values every gift.

But we can go much further than that. Just think about how we want our contributions to church to be recognized and praised. I so easily and quickly fish for compliments. My standard technique is to comment on something I've done saying how rubbish it was, hoping that people will be prompted into correcting me. 'No, it was great,' they'll say, and I'll feel good.

Just think about how we play the comparison game. We compare ourselves with others and hope we come out better, feeling good about ourselves if we do and worse if we don't. We may make critical comments about other people to do them down and elevate ourselves. In my worst moments, I find myself hoping other people aren't very good speakers – compared to me, that is. Whereas what I should be doing is rejoicing in their gifting.

We can so easily play a Christianized version of the ladders of the world. I worry where I am on the ladder compared to everyone else. It might be my role in the church, my up-front profile, being known to serve, being thought of as good at hospitality, caring for people, great at evangelism, or whatever. The key thing is that I derive my sense of identity from my assessment of those things.

And this is in the life of the church where I and others are supposed to know who we are in Christ! We are brothers and sisters sitting round God's table, equally loved and valuable to him. And so we must jump off the Christian ladders we find ourselves climbing just as much as the 'worldly' ladders of fashion, appearance, and career.

Attitudes to one another

Think about our attitude to and acceptance of one another. If we see ourselves as freely forgiven, then we will try to forgive others. If I see myself as deeply loved, I will give myself to loving others. If I see myself as having been sacrificially served, I will work at serving others. If I see myself as having been treated graciously, I will strive to be gracious to others. This link between how God has treated us in Christ and our treatment of others is made explicit by Paul. Here are two examples:

Accept one another as Christ accepted you. (Romans 15:7)

Forgive one another as the Lord forgave you. (Colossians 3:13)

This means that our knowledge of how Christ has treated us is to flow over to others. Our identity as accepted and forgiven is not simply to be revelled in, but to influence how we treat those around us.

So think now of the evaluations we make of other people: the comments and impressions we give them about themselves, the acceptance or rejection we offer, the attitude of welcome or of exclusion we can give off. In the church we can so easily admire those who have a successful professional career rather than those whose work is menial or home-based. We can prefer the good-looking and the gifted, the popular and the pleasant. Through what we do, who we ask to fulfil important roles, and how we talk about it, we send messages. And we have to ask ourselves what message we are sending: are we reflecting God's view of us or reinforcing worldly self-image thinking?

Imagine if someone walks into your church and finds warm acceptance no matter how 'acceptable' they are. Imagine if everyone is valued and affirmed, no matter what abilities they have or don't have. Imagine if everyone is treated equally, no matter what skeletons they have in their closet. Imagine if forgiveness is freely extended to all, rather than to some and only on certain conditions. This is the culture of a group of people who know who they are in Christ and so are not operating on the old identity rules of the world.

Feedback loops

The great thing about such a culture is that it works in a sort of positive feedback loop; it helps us realize who we are in Christ. Just think about it. Think what happens when I am forgiven freely by others in church, or accepted unconditionally despite who I am. That gives me a demonstration of how God has treated me. It is a horizontal working out of my identity with other people that flows from the vertical truth of my identity with God. It reminds me of that and so it helps me to think rightly of myself, to have a biblical self-image. That is what is pictured in the illustration below.

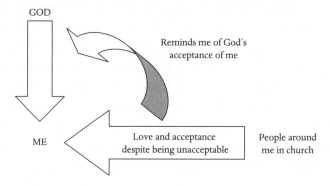

But just think what happens if a church culture plays the worldly game of identity in a Christian guise, where my acceptance all depends on what I can offer, how cool I am, my appearance or my performance. What will I learn from my experience of church? All it will do is reinforce my tendency to gain my identity from such sources.

It will confirm me in my need to play the game and it will undermine any teaching about God's acceptance of me. I can sit in church and be told I am loved despite being unlovable, but never experience that horizontally from people. That means it remains a nice idea with no reality to it. Of course the love and acceptance of those around me in the church will never be all that it should be. But it should still reflect God's wonderful love and acceptance of us, and it will help us realize the reality of that.

Somewhere I can be a sinner

This culture of knowing who we are in Christ will mean that we can be honest about our sinfulness. Honesty here will remind and help each of us to face up to our sin – and to rejoice in forgiveness. But so often churches establish a culture where being a sinner is like a theoretical idea we all say we agree with but never speak honestly about. This is to wear masks with each other and so play the image game.

Imagine a church where sinfulness is treated straightforwardly. People speak as if every sin were a very real possibility for them because they know the state of their hearts; no one looks down on others for having fallen into really 'bad' sin. The German pastor and theologian Dietrich Bonhoeffer said:

> In the presence of a psychiatrist I can only be a sick man; in the presence of a Christian brother I can dare to be a sinner.

There is a real issue here, because the average church can give off the impression of being strong and sorted as opposed to sinful and struggling. People look round and everyone else *seems* happy, content and victorious, and so they feel like this is the last place where they could share their real feelings and struggles.

In the church, of all places, people should be helped to see themselves as God would want them to. This of course means that sin is never ignored and that standards are held high. But it also means that grace is celebrated and forgiveness is practised. What a different and what an attractive community that is.

All this is also true in the Christian home and so should profoundly influence Christian parenting. But that would be another book, and we need to move on to some practical steps.

Questions for reflection or discussion

1. In what way are we to return to the pattern of creation in our relationship with God and in our relationship with other people?

2. What fundamental change in attitude is needed for this to happen?
3. How do you feel about the idea of needing people less and loving people more?
4. What implications should our biblical identity have in the life of the church? Describe things that you think should and should not happen.
5. What particular implications are there for how we talk about sin and about forgiveness as Christians? In what ways can these be distorted in church life?

9. working it out

Time to get practical. We've described our attempts at creating and preserving our identity. We each do this in slightly different ways but we all look in the mirrors of success, status, appearance and so on. Above all, we value other people's opinions and want to be seen to be cool or clever or successful or fun.

This is part of our culture – and it's a part that we have simply absorbed. Paul wrote to the Christians in Rome, telling them about how to live in a non-Christian world:

> Do not conform to the pattern of this world, but be transformed by the renewing of your mind. (Romans 12:2)

See the idea? We can so easily be conformists who run along with whatever those around us are doing, but we must resist that and think differently. Some areas will be fairly obvious: for example, I know that my culture's view of sex or money is different from how God would want me to think about it. I need to renew my mind there. But at least I can see the challenge to conform and can fight against it.

The problem comes when I don't even realize there is a pressure to conform and am shaped without even realizing it. I think that's the case with identity. Our culture tells us how we should go about creating our identity and we follow suit. We are told about thinking well of ourselves, being concerned with our image and comparing ourselves to those around us. And we go along with it. Everyone plays the game and we join in without even asking.

We need to be transformed by the renewing of our minds. I hope some of that renewal has happened as you have read this book. In this chapter we're going to try to work through that process more practically.

Review time

Let's review where we've got to. I hope you've seen that we:

- were created with the humble dignity of the image of God;
- are truly guilty and shameful in our rebellion against God;
- are restored to a position of dignity and honour in Christ; we are accepted despite being unacceptable and so are forever secure as God's children;
- now have the humble dignity of living to obey and serve God while staying in the grace of God;
- live a re-orientated life where Christ is at the centre; we live to glorify him and to love other people.

It's worth comparing this identity that we see in the mirror of God's word with what we will have if we look in the mirrors of the world around us. The table below summarizes the differences:

Mirror of the world	Mirror of God's word
Distorted picture of myself	True picture of myself
Fluctuating view of myself with circumstances and / or situations	Stable view of myself
Depends on comparison with others or my performance	Depends on God's declaration
Overall feeling of insecurity	Overall feeling of security
Need other people or threatened by them	Free to love and serve other people
Worried and unsure about who I am	Assured of who I am
Life revolves around me, my importance, my glory	Life revolves around Jesus, his importance, his glory
Focus on me, my performance, what I do and achieve	Focus on God and all that he has done and continues to do for me

What a difference it makes! The question is how we move from one column to the other; how we stop looking in the mirrors of the world and only look in the mirror of God's word. We're going to try to develop a sort of personal action plan. And then we'll think in more detail about some of the areas in which we struggle most often.

Personal action plan

I'd encourage you not simply to read this section but actually to go through the process described. We've said a few times that this is not an issue we solve overnight. Each of us will have to do some reflecting for ourselves and that is what this section is all about.

It is worth beginning with some diagnostic questions. These are simply to help us see how we tend to operate – which mirrors we tend to look in and what is important to our identity. Here they are:

- What do I do specifically to be liked or thought well of?
- How would I feel if my appearance was different?
- Why do I tend to feel good about myself?
- Why do I tend to feel bad about myself?
- What would I change about myself if I could? What difference do I think that would make?
- What am I proud of? Why?
- What, if removed, would shake my view of myself?

If you have answered these questions, you should have a pretty good idea about where you tend to look for your identity or self-image. I hope, having read through this book, you will know yourself better and what your identity-building strategy is. I hope you are also committed to laying your own strategy aside and developing a biblical view of yourself. I hope you long to grow in realization of your humble dignity in Christ and live a re-orientated life.

I think of that process of change as a two-part process. We must combat the negative: that is, we must be honest regarding how we tend to look in the wrong mirror, and must take steps to stop doing so. But we must also reinforce the positive: that is, we must develop a right biblical identity and take steps to keep on looking in the right mirror.

Here's a flow diagram for each step.

Combating the negative

Which 'mirrors' do I tend to look in for my self-image?
(e.g. appearance, performance, opinions, background)

Why do I do this?
(e.g. something in my upbringing; my situation; my culture;
my friends; my personality; my talents; my opportunities)

How should I respond to this area of my life?
How does God want me to think about it?
What truths should I remind myself of?

What practical steps can I take to avoid
looking in this mirror?
What practical steps can I take to counteract
the effect this has?
(e.g. not fishing for compliments; 'deliberately dressing
down'; being careful which magazines I read or what TV I
watch; avoiding certain conversations with friends;
consciously critiquing adverts I see; deliberately praising
others I would usually feel envious of)

I hope that process is fairly clear. We want to reflect on what
we currently do and then ask how God would want us to

think, and respond differently. We need to renew our minds on issues of success and beauty and so on. We'll think more about that below. But we must also end up with some practical steps to avoid looking in our particular mirrors. Personally I need to stop fishing for compliments and avoid conversations that put others down so I can feel better about myself.

But combating the negative is not enough. We must also have the positive humble dignity that God wants us to have.

Reinforcing the positive

Realize who I am in Christ
(Which aspects of my humble dignity in Christ do
I tend to forget? How do I tend to think of my identity as a
Christian? What do I need to remind myself of?)

What prevents me believing/living out this truth?
(e.g. lack of understanding; unwillingness to believe
God; pride)

How does God want me to respond?
Do I need to be reassured / encouraged / rebuked /
humbled / taught?

What practical steps can I take so that this truth sinks in?
(e.g. memorization of Bible verses; particular focus in
prayers; encouragement of others; Bible study on certain
topics; asking friends to keep me accountable and remind
me of truth)

Again, I hope the process is clear. The main aim of this book
has been to establish the humble dignity that is ours in Christ.
We need to think through where we don't believe or embrace
that, and ask ourselves why. And then we must respond with
practical steps. Personally, I must remind myself of God's
holiness and my sin so I stop thinking of myself as a nice
bloke. So I plan to memorize a couple of verses on this and
ask some close friends to check up on me.

Living in the real world

Let's consider some of the key areas where we all tend to
struggle and where we need to renew our minds from the patterns of thinking that will be deeply engrained in us.

Praise or criticism

How should I think about and respond to praise or criticism?
It might be over the quality of my work, my cooking, my DIY,
my children, or my music or anything I do. It is often about
things I say and do for others – I am commended for my kindness or thoughtfulness or appropriateness. Or I am ticked off
for my carelessness, sarcasm or lack of tact.

I can think of being 'told off' at work by a senior colleague
for my attitude to an area of work which I thought was a
waste of time. I can think of my occasional unkind words
being pointed out by my wife. I can think of criticism of
my sermons. And equally, I can think of moments of praise
in all those areas. I hate the criticism and I love the praise!

Most of us do. We want to be thought well of by those around us.

We should recognize that certain patterns of upbringing in our childhood can increase this tendency. One of the most common is where criticism was the order of the day: constant comments from parents about what wasn't right and what could be improved, being treated as if nothing we did was very good, or worse, being teased or ridiculed.

Life like this means you feel that you are constantly being disapproved of and you can respond by longing for praise. You angle all you do so that it is seen in the best light and hope you will get commendation for it. As with all of our backgrounds, it is helpful to recognize what effects there may have been, but we remain responsible for how we react now.

How should we renew our minds here? Let me make some suggestions.

We need to remind ourselves that, in Christ and by his Spirit, we can now do things that do deserve praise. We thought about this in an earlier chapter on our obedience and serving God. When we are kind or thoughtful, or when we do something well, there is nothing wrong with someone saying 'Well done!' or 'Thank you', and we can be genuinely pleased they have done so.

But we must also remind ourselves of the humility involved. I can only do something worthy of praise because of God having renewed me, gifted me and now working through me by his Spirit. So while I am involved, it is not all down to me! When I am praised, I can't say to myself in response, 'Aren't I brilliant?' But I can say, 'Thank you God for working through me and giving me the ability to live in a way that loves you and loves other people.'

When we are criticized it may be that the criticism is unfair. And we should humbly defend ourselves. More of an issue is when the criticism is good and right – we may have done something badly when it should have been better, or we may have done something wrong or unkind. Such moments remind us of our sin. And we should expect this to happen. Rebukes from those around us are one of the ways God will work to renew us. Proverbs 27:6 says, 'Wounds from a friend can be trusted, but an enemy multiplies kisses.'

I ended up talking to Ali about this just today. He said that a friend had recently brought him up short with a couple of areas he thought Ali should be aware of and sort out. It was a gentle but firm rebuke. Ali said he felt shattered by such criticism. And then he said, 'But I know I'm a sinner, and all this did was remind me that I'm a sinner, so why I am so surprised and so shattered?' It was a good observation. We talked about it and agreed that although we 'know' we are sinners, we actually still harbour nice thoughts about ourselves. And we rest some of our image and security on being 'nice'.

In other words, we lose sight of the fact of our sin, stop trusting in grace and move to think we can offer God something ourselves. It's not as worked out as that in our heads, but that can be what's going on. Then when someone criticizes us our whole ground of identity is shattered – we are not who we thought we were.

And so, if I am criticized and the criticism is fair, I must let it remind me of my sin and that I have nothing in myself to trust in. I must allow it to push me to repentance and confession and sorrow that I am grieving God. And I must remind myself and rejoice that I am secure in Christ.

And most fundamentally in all of this, I say to myself that left to myself I deserve no praise at all, but only just and right condemnation. But Christ has obeyed on my behalf and been condemned on my behalf. While I can now live pleasing or displeasing God, ultimately *there is no criticism for me but only praise if I am in Christ.*

Success or failure

How should I think about and respond to my successes or my failures in life? They come in all shapes and sizes. It might be my academic qualifications, my sporting achievements, a job or a promotion, or winning a competition I entered. Or failure at those things and more.

This area is similar to the one above. It's just that above we focused on other people's opinions of what I've done, whereas this focuses on a more objective achievement. There's a line of some kind and I have either passed or failed to pass it so that I think I have succeeded or failed.

This area appeals particularly to wanting to 'prove yourself'. A friend of mine talks about the film *Toy Story* where Buzz Lightyear thinks he can really fly. He can't and doesn't, he just bounces around the room in a vague imitation of flying. But when he lands he announces triumphantly, 'Can!' My friend says we can simply want the satisfaction of saying with Buzz, 'Can!' It's the desire to say, 'I can do it, I've proved myself.'

We should recognize that this can often stem from an upbringing where achievement was held to be very important. Parents were interested in exam results and expressed pleasure or displeasure, all depending on the mark. Or they were very concerned about achievement in music or sport, and smiled or frowned depending on the relative success or failure. That can instil in us a desire to prove ourselves. Again, we remain responsible for how we live now with such a background, but recognizing it can help in understanding ourselves and responding differently.

How should we renew our minds here? A few thoughts.

I should remember God's gifting and God's enabling in all of life. All my abilities come from him, whether abilities at teaching the Bible, kicking a football, playing the piano or painting a picture. More than that, I must remember my gifts are given for the glory of God and the good of others as I serve them. And so my response to success must include thankfulness to God. I should say, 'Thank you that I have these abilities and I can live in your creation doing these things well.' And I look to use my gifts for the benefit of those around me and am pleased when God uses me to help others.

In my failures, I should remember that other people are gifted as well. My failing often means someone else succeeding instead – they got the job instead of me – and so I rejoice that others have greater abilities than me, and remind myself that my strengths may lie elsewhere.

I may also have to tell myself that some failures are my fault. Maybe I didn't work hard enough, or practise enough. Failure is sometimes the result of sin. At which point I need to be honest with myself and confess it to God. And remind myself that I stand in grace – this failure doesn't mean I'm no longer accepted by God.

But sometimes failure is no one's fault particularly – just a combination of circumstances. We live in a world where, because of sin, the whole world doesn't work as it was supposed to. We get ill, computers crash, recipes go wrong, and things break. We were created to be rulers of the world under God, but that is frustrated because of sin and so we cannot and will not succeed at all we do.

And so I must remember that this world is not as it is supposed to be. And so I should also remind myself of the difference between true and false shame. Many of my failures are not my fault even if others look down on me for them. I must not make the expectations of others around me the standard that judges me.

In all of this, I remember that success or failure changes nothing about who I am. My humble dignity in Christ remains secure. More fundamentally I must remember my sin means that I couldn't prove myself worthy even if I wanted to, but that Jesus has done everything for me. *There is nothing for me to prove to anyone if I am in Christ.*

Living in relationships

How should I feel about my relationships? For most people, this will mainly be with friends, but for many it will also be with family and maybe a spouse. We are thinking here, not of their praise or criticism as we did above, but the rather vaguer area of their *love*. It might be vague but it is huge! I want to feel loved, liked, accepted, welcomed. Call it whatever you like, but I want it. And as a result I am so easily a people pleaser because I want people to like me.

All sorts of issues in upbringing can come into play here. Especially common is when we haven't felt that we received a great deal of love. Parents may have been caring enough but not very affectionate. This can result in us thinking that we are not very lovable and then we can go out of our way to get people to like us and express love to us. Or it can be that we only ever received affection when we did something for someone. Unless we performed well we received the message that we weren't lovable. This can easily result in an inability to say no to anything because we think meeting other people's expectations is what means they will like us.

How should we renew our minds here?

We need to remember something about how God created us. We were created to live not only in relationship with God, but also in loving community with those around us. This is part of what God made us for. As a result, this is a hard area to get the right perspective on. Sometimes people say that if we know God loves us it shouldn't matter what love we receive from people around us because we are secure in God. But this view ignores that we have been created to live in relationships with people as well as God. We don't live in a bubble with just me and God and no one else. And so a lack of loving relationships will hurt, and we should expect it to hurt. This is why something like solitary confinement is the punishment that it is.

I don't mean to say that security in our relationship with God makes no difference when we do not have good relationships – of course it does. But I am saying we shouldn't pretend that we can take or leave relationships as if they don't matter to us. That is to deny how we were created. The problem comes when we look to those relationships as our source of identity, when we become dependent in them and look to other people as a source of affirmation.

So I should remind myself that relationships are a good part of creation but that they are so often distorted by sin. If someone is rude, hurtful or unkind and I feel rejected or unloved, that may well be because that person is being sinful.

However I must beware of living for people's love. I must watch out for thoughts that say, 'If only he or she or they liked me more, then life would be OK.' I must tell myself that I should be more concerned to love them, than worry about whether they love me.

In fact I should go further and remind myself that my sin means I am not intrinsically lovable. I hide parts of myself from people specifically so that they will continue to like me. If they knew what I was really like, who'd want to be my friend? There are, of course, some who do know my failures and continue to love me anyway and I thank God for them (I thank God for my wife in this!). In those relationships I see a reflection of God's love which is truly unconditional.

But it is God's love that I should dwell on most: God is the one who has loved me despite all my unloveliness. He has loved me with an amazing, costly, deep and rich love. He loved me when I least deserved it and had done nothing to ask for it. And so his love doesn't depend on me. I don't have to worry about whether it will stop or run out. *I am wonderfully loved in Christ.*

Our appearance

The designer Ben Sherman proudly said, 'Looking good isn't important; looking good is everything.' That's certainly what our culture believes. Whether it is body image, beauty or fashion, we all know instinctively what's wanted and valued. Here perhaps more than anywhere else, our culture subtly shapes us and seeps into us.

Advertising tells us what 'beautiful' is, or is supposed to be, and deliberately sets out to make people feel dissatisfied with the way they look. We can buy into the gym, diet and tan culture that aims for the perfect body. We can spend money on fashionable clothes. We read about makeovers in magazines. We watch TV programmes that take someone who is unhappy with who they are and their life, and are shown how a change in appearance and clothing transforms them.

Our upbringing can of course come into play here as well. If we kept hearing comments about how pretty we looked, or what a great impression we will make, we will have learnt to think about our appearance in a certain way. Equally, being told we are fat or ugly will have had its effect. Of course this doesn't have to be from parents; kids start to hear these comments (usually the negative ones) from an early age from their peers.

How should we renew our minds here? Here are some ideas.

We need to remind ourselves that such a thing as physical outward beauty does exist. The Bible recognizes that some people are more beautiful or attractive than others (for example Esther 1:11; 2:7 and 2 Samuel 14:25). And there is no embarrassment about delighting in the beauty of a wife or a husband (see Song of Songs 1:15; 5:10–16). In addition there is not necessarily a problem with wearing decent clothes, jewellery, or make-up (see Song of Songs 1:10–11). In other words we don't deny the reality of beauty and can make ourselves more or less attractive (a least a bit).

But we must tell ourselves that God is concerned with inner beauty. He looks on people's hearts and is pleased or displeased with what he finds there. And so we should be much more concerned with our godliness than our hairstyle. We should pour more energy into our character makeover than our beauty makeover.

This is the warning that Peter gives to women in particular, although the same idea runs true for blokes:

> Your beauty should not come from outward adornment, such as elaborate hairstyles and the wearing of gold jewellery and fine clothes. Rather it should be that of your inner self, the unfading beauty of a gentle and quiet spirit which is of great worth in God's sight. (1 Peter 3:3–4)

It's pretty clear, isn't it? We should strive for beauty of character. Notice that Peter mentions that the inner beauty he is talking about is 'unfading'. I think he is reflecting on what a temporary thing outer beauty is. Even if you think you cut it in the beauty stakes now, just give it a few years. And of course those who have defined themselves by how they look are then most desperate about not losing their looks. They are the ones who throw themselves into cosmetics and surgery, desperately hoping to preserve their standing. What foolishness.

We must also realize what a prime category this is for false shame. Many, many people have a poor body image simply because it doesn't match what our culture tells us a good body is. Models who are unhealthily thin, cosmetically enhanced and airbrushed to perfection are held up as the ideal. Who can compete? And so this is a false thing to feel shamefaced about. This is not a moral category!

But we must go further and tell ourselves that our attempts at looking good on the outside can so easily be attempts at hiding what we know is on the inside. I know my moral ugliness, but if I can pass myself off as physically attractive or cool, people won't know about what I'm really like. In fact I'll deceive myself about it too.

So I should come clean and admit than no beauty product or item of clothing can cover my shame. But then I remind myself that Jesus can and he does. The author Amelia Clarke writes this specifically to women:

> Don't spend all your time and money pursuing that fat-free, full-lipped, tummy tucked, muscle toned, pencil-eyebrowed, smooth-skinned, chisel-cheeked size 6. You are a princess, already fabulous, designed and loved by God.

Remind yourself what is true of you in Christ, what he has done for you and how he made you. *I have been truly made beautiful in Jesus.*

Renew your mind

In all these ways and more we need to renew our thinking so that we do not conform to the pattern of the world. This is hard work. It involves careful thinking and is best done in community, with the teaching, encouragement and support of others. But it must be done. We need to know who we are in Christ and be able to live that out in the real world of success and criticism, blame and beauty. But praise God that the humble dignity we have in Jesus can withstand the pressures of the real world – we can be free of these things, confident of who we are in Jesus.

Questions for reflection or discussion

1. In what ways do you think we've been 'conformed to the pattern of the world' with regard to identity?
2. Work through the two steps of the personal action plan above. What has struck you? What practical steps can you take?
3. Which of the areas of praise or criticism, success or failure, living in relationships, or appearance struck you most? Why?
4. What change would you most like to see in your thinking in these areas?
5. How will you continue to live out your humble dignity in Christ in the real world? What pressures do you know you will face? How will you respond?

conclusion

By my rebellion I am not what I was supposed to be.
By God's wonderful grace I am not what I was.
By that same grace I will one day be what God intended.

We will keep on wrestling with this identity stuff for the rest of our lives. It's part of Christian discipleship that we are going to have to keep on working out in practice. Praise God that through his word and Spirit we can know who we are and can discover and live out the freedom and dignity of who we were meant to be. But with a sinful heart and in a sinful world it will always be a struggle – we will keep on being tempted to define ourselves in sinful ways.

But one day we will be re-created along with the rest of the physical world. The new creation that God has started in us will be completed. The work of the Spirit in changing us will be over. Then I will know truly and completely who I am in Christ. Then I will be what I was meant to be. Then I will love God with all my heart and love those around me as myself. Then I will be focused on Jesus and living for him and his glory.

And when that transformation happens, I'll never fish for compliments again. I'll never worry over what people think of what I just said. I'll never ask myself whether I'm liked or loved or accepted. I'll never reassure myself with my achievements or despair over my failures. I'll never do anything for the sake of appearance. I'll never fret over my appearance or weight. I'll never wish I could change something about me or want to be someone else.

Come, Lord Jesus, come.

notes

notes

Chapter 1 Looking in the mirror

p. 16   <http://www.rapidnet.com/~jbeard/bdm/Psychology/self-est/self.htm>.

p. 16   James Dobson, *What Wives Wish Their Husbands Knew About Women* (Tyndale House Publishers, 1981), p. 35.

p. 17   Edward Welch, *When People are Big and God is Small* (P & R Publishing, 1997), p. 17.

p. 18   Welch, *When People are Big and God is Small*, p. 17.

p. 20   Quoted in Andrew Bonar, *The Life of Robert Murray M'Cheyne* (Banner of Truth, 1960), pp. 23–24.

p. 23   John Calvin, *Institutes of the Christian Religion*, Book 2, Chapter 2.11.

Chapter 2 Taking the lid off

p. 38   <http://yourtotalhealth.ivillage.com/diet-fitness/boost-your-confidence.html>.

p. 39   Chris Heath, *Feel: Robbie Williams* (Ebury Press, 2004).

p. 41   Jay Adams, *The Biblical View of Self-Esteem, Self-Love, Self-Image* (Harvest House Publishers, 1986), p. 106.

Chapter 3 The original design

p. 45   Calvin, *Institutes*, Book 1, Chapter 1.1.

p. 50   Henri Blocher, *In the Beginning: The Opening Chapters of Genesis* (IVP, 1984).

Chapter 4 The shameful admission

p. 63   William Orme, *The Practical Works of The Rev. Richard Baxter with a Life of the Author* (London, 1830), p. xvi.

p. 63   Quoted in Bonar, *The Life of Robert Murray M'Cheyne*, p. 26.

p. 63   Dick Keyes, *Beyond Identity: Finding Your Way in the Image and Character of God* (Paternoster Press, 1998), pp. 51–52.

p. 65   C. S. Lewis, *Mere Christianity* (Collins, 1986), p. 109.

p. 67   Keyes, *Beyond Identity*, p. 41.

Chapter 5 The new beginning

p. 79   Anthony Hoekema, *The Christian Looks at Himself* (Eerdmans, 1975), pp. 56–57.

p. 81   Martin Luther, *Christ Delighting in the Beauty of the Righteous*, translated by H. Cole (W. Simkin & R. Marshall, 1826), I. 281.

Chapter 6 Accepting acceptance

p. 88   Walter Trobisch, *Love Yourself* (IVP, 1976), p. 11.

p. 90   Randy Alcorn, <http://www.epm.org/articles/psyself.html>.

p. 91   Robert Schuller, 'Hard Questions for Robert Schuller about Sin and Self-Esteem', *Christianity Today* 28, August 1984.

p. 91   David Powlison, 'Idols of the Heart and "Vanity Fair" ', *Journal of Biblical Counselling*, 13/2, 1995.

p. 92   Paul Tillich, *The Courage To Be* (Collins, 1962), p. 160.

Chapter 7 Living the new life

p. 115   Joanna McGrath and Alister McGrath, *The Dilemma of Self-Esteem: The Cross and Christian Confidence* (Crossway Books, 1992), p. 145.

Chapter 8 The re-orientated life

p. 121   Lewis, *Mere Christianity*, p. 188.

p. 131   Dietrich Bonhoeffer, *Life Together* (Harper & Row, 1954), p. 119.

Chapter 9 Working it out

p. 148   Amelia Clarke, 'Self-Esteem and God's Esteem', *The Briefing*, 285,
          June 2002.

a **lively** introduction

to **biblical** teaching

about the **Holy Spirit**

Experiencing the Spirit

New Testament essentials for every Christian

ivp

GRAHAM BEYNON

For some Christians, God the Holy Spirit is something of a mystery, and they are not too sure what to say about him. Others speak with confidence and enthusiasm about him, challenging us to be 'filled with the Spirit', or to live a 'Spirit-filled life'. As a result, the work of the Spirit has sometimes been controversial.

The three members of the Godhead – Father, Son and Holy Spirit – are not only distinct persons; they also have distinct roles. Graham Beynon looks at the main New Testament passages in which the Spirit's work is described. With freshness and clarity, he builds a picture of what the Holy Spirit does, and hence what experiencing him in our lives should look like.

'I found this book really encouraging ... I'd recommend it to any Christian who wants to think more and have a broad perspective on the work of the Spirit'
a satisfied IVP reader